Holistic Healing For Pets
How to Care for Your Pet Through Holistic and Alternative Healing
Ruby Watson

Copyright © Vellaz Publishing 2022

All rights reserved.
No part of this book may be reproduced by any means without written permission from the copyright holder.

Cover image © Vellaz Studio
Review by Armando Vellaz
Graphic design by Amadeu Brumm
Layout by Matheus Costa
All rights reserved to: Vellaz Publishing

Holism

Summary

Prologue 5
Chapter 1 Holistic Treatments for Pets 7
Chapter 2 Vital Energy and the Connection with Animals 15
Chapter 3 Massage Techniques to Calm and Revitalize 23
Chapter 4 Aromatherapy Using Essential Oils for Pet Well-Being
.... 32
Chapter 5 Reiki for Animals Channeling Energy for Healing 41
Chapter 6 Chromotherapy The Power of Colors in Animal Health
.... 48
Chapter 7 Balancing Chakras and Energies 54
Chapter 8 Natural Diet and the Connection to Energetic Well-Being 62
Chapter 9 Music Therapy Healing Sounds 71
Chapter 10 Breathing and Meditation Techniques with Pets 80
Chapter 11 Using Medicinal Plants 88
Chapter 12 Bach Flower Remedies and Other Vibrational Essences 97
Chapter 13 Balancing Animal Chakras Focus on the Root Chakra 106
Chapter 14 Balancing Animal Chakras 115
Chapter 15 Focus on the Solar Plexus Chakra 125
Chapter 16 Focus on the Heart Chakra 135
Chapter 17 Focus on the Throat Chakra 144
Chapter 18 Focus on the Third Eye Chakra 153
Chapter 19 Focus on the Crown Chakra 162

Chapter 20 Vibrational Frequencies for Healing 170

Chapter 21 Homeopathy for Animals 179

Chapter 22 Reflexology for Animals: Healing Through Feet and Paws 189

Chapter 23 Multidimensional Healing Integrating Multiple Holistic Therapies 199

Epilogue 209

Prologue

There is an invisible and profound world that connects you to your pet, a silent bond filled with meaning and emotion. It's a symphony of feelings, energies, and gestures, where every stroke, glance, or breath creates a flow of love that transcends the physical. Right now, you have the opportunity to explore a dimension of this relationship you may never have considered before. What if I told you that within this book lie secrets capable of transforming the way you care for and communicate with your loyal companion? That here are keys to unlocking complete health, not just for your pet's body, but for their mind and spirit?

Prepare yourself for a journey of discovery. Imagine if, instead of merely treating symptoms, you could understand what lies behind your pet's behaviors and physical signs? Through ancient practices such as Reiki, chromotherapy, and aromatherapy, you will not only provide comfort but also emotional and energetic balance, nourishing your pet in a way that goes beyond conventional care.

Holistic healing is more than an approach; it is a philosophy of life that places your pet's well-being at the center of a universe of integrated care. As you dive into the pages of this book, you will awaken a new perception, where you will understand that your pet's well-being reflects your own energy. Your pet feels your vibrations, your emotions, and responds to them more deeply than the eyes can perceive.

Have you ever imagined being able to restore your pet's emotional and energetic balance with a simple touch? Or how the gentle melody of music can calm even the most hectic days? This is not some distant, esoteric mystery; it is real, tangible, and within your reach. This book will guide you with practical steps to apply healing techniques that are natural, non-invasive, and deeply transformative.

Science has already shown that animals are energetically connected to their surroundings, absorbing the energies around them. This means that your emotional state can directly affect your pet's health and behavior. So, by exploring the techniques this book offers, you will also find yourself on a journey of self-healing. By balancing your home's energy, and your own, you are contributing to your companion's integral well-being.

Allow yourself to go beyond the obvious. Open your mind to a universe of possibilities where healing does not need to come from heavy medications or invasive solutions, but can be found in the harmony between body, mind, and spirit. Here, you will discover that the right touch, a soothing fragrance, or the correct color can work wonders for your pet's balance.

So, what are you waiting for? Let yourself be carried away by this experience. Awaken to the understanding that your pet is not just an animal by your side, but an energetic being, a soul that, like you, seeks peace, balance, and health. Get ready for surprising revelations that will forever change the way you care for your companion. Here is the invitation to transform their life—and yours—in a profound, harmonious, and lasting way.

Chapter 1
Holistic Treatments for Pets

Holistic treatments for pets focus on nurturing the entire being—body, mind, and spirit—by considering not just the physical health of an animal but also their emotional and energetic well-being. The philosophy behind holistic care is that the animal's health should be approached as a whole, where all aspects are interconnected. This comprehensive perspective allows pet owners to better understand their pets' needs beyond conventional veterinary care, offering a complementary pathway to achieving long-term health, happiness, and vitality.

In recent years, pet owners have become increasingly aware of how these holistic approaches can complement traditional veterinary treatments. Instead of simply treating symptoms, holistic therapies work to identify and address the root causes of health issues, aiming to restore balance in the pet's body and energy systems. This integration can be particularly helpful in managing chronic conditions, improving recovery times, and enhancing the overall quality of life for animals. Many of these therapies, such as acupuncture, massage, aromatherapy, and energy healing, are based on centuries-old practices adapted to meet the specific needs of animals.

At the heart of holistic treatment lies the concept of energy balance. Just as in humans, the flow of energy in animals is vital to their overall well-being. Energy flows through pathways in the body, known in some traditions as meridians, and interacts with various energy centers. In this context, illness or behavioral issues in pets are often viewed as imbalances or blockages in these energy flows. When energy is disrupted—whether by stress, injury, or emotional distress—it can lead to both physical and mental health issues. Holistic therapies aim to restore the natural flow of this energy, promoting healing and preventing future imbalances.

One key principle in holistic pet care is recognizing that animals experience emotions and mental states similar to humans. Pets, whether they are dogs, cats, horses, or even smaller creatures, can suffer from stress, anxiety, and depression. These emotional states are not separate from their physical health. For example, an anxious dog might develop digestive issues, or a stressed cat could start grooming excessively to the point of harming its skin. By addressing the emotional well-being of a pet, holistic therapies seek to improve both mental health and physical symptoms, recognizing the profound connection between the two.

Holistic pet care often involves a combination of treatments, each designed to work in harmony with the animal's natural healing mechanisms. These treatments can include dietary adjustments, energy healing practices like Reiki, herbal medicine, massage, acupuncture, and even mindfulness practices shared between the owner and pet. Importantly, holistic approaches are not a replacement for conventional veterinary medicine but rather a complement that enhances and supports traditional treatments. For example, a dog recovering from surgery might benefit from acupuncture to reduce pain and inflammation, while a cat with chronic anxiety may find relief through aromatherapy combined with behavioral modifications.

Pet owners seeking holistic treatments for their animals often begin by exploring natural remedies that can reduce the need for pharmaceuticals or invasive procedures. Many conventional treatments, while effective, can have side effects that holistic therapies may help mitigate. For instance, medications prescribed for chronic conditions can sometimes cause digestive upset, fatigue, or mood changes in pets. Holistic approaches offer an alternative by encouraging the body's own ability to heal. This might involve the use of herbal supplements to support digestion, massage to reduce muscle tension, or chromotherapy to stimulate energy flow and soothe anxiety.

The relationship between pet and owner plays a crucial role in holistic healing. This bond is an essential part of the therapeutic process. Animals are highly sensitive to the emotions and energies of their human companions, and when a pet owner is stressed, anxious, or emotionally unbalanced, it can have a direct impact on the pet's well-being. Holistic treatments often encourage the owner to participate actively in the healing process. By fostering a calm, positive environment, pet owners can contribute to their animals' recovery and emotional balance. This shared journey of healing strengthens the bond, creating a deeper level of understanding and trust.

An important aspect of holistic pet care is the idea of prevention. By maintaining an animal's overall health and energetic balance, holistic therapies can help prevent illness before it starts. For instance, regular energy balancing sessions like Reiki can keep an animal's energy centers aligned, reducing the likelihood of stress-related illnesses. Additionally, a balanced, natural diet rich in essential nutrients can support the immune system, preventing chronic conditions from developing. Exercise, mental stimulation, and emotional enrichment also play a role in preventive care, as they help maintain a pet's physical and mental health over time.

Holistic treatments are as much about creating a nurturing, supportive environment for the pet as they are about specific therapies. The physical space where a pet lives—whether it's a home, yard, or stable—can significantly impact their health. Factors such as noise levels, exposure to natural light, access to fresh air, and the presence of calming elements like plants or water features can all influence an animal's sense of well-being. Creating a peaceful, secure environment for a pet is a key part of holistic care. This space should be free from unnecessary stressors and filled with positive energy that encourages relaxation and healing.

Holistic approaches also acknowledge the individuality of each animal. Just as no two people are the same, pets have unique physical, emotional, and energetic needs. One dog may respond well to massage, while another may find acupuncture more beneficial. The goal of holistic care is to tailor treatments to the specific needs of the animal, observing their responses to different therapies and adjusting the approach as necessary. This personalized care enhances the effectiveness of treatments, ensuring that the animal's unique needs are met.

Holistic pet care is grounded in the belief that pets, like humans, are more than just their physical bodies. They are beings with their own emotions, personalities, and energy fields. By respecting and nurturing all aspects of their being, holistic therapies aim to create a state of harmony and balance, leading to a healthier, happier life for the pet. Whether through energy healing, natural remedies, or the power of a strong human-animal bond, these treatments offer a pathway to deeper well-being and longevity for our beloved animal companions.

Holistic care for pets encompasses a wide range of modalities, each rooted in the idea of balancing the body's energy and promoting natural healing. In this continuation of our exploration into holistic treatments, we will delve deeper into several of the most prominent and effective practices—acupuncture, aromatherapy, chromotherapy, and Reiki—and their energetic foundations. By understanding how these therapies work and how to apply them, pet owners can help improve their pets' health, behavior, and emotional well-being in meaningful ways.

Acupuncture is perhaps one of the most well-known holistic modalities, derived from traditional Chinese medicine. The practice involves inserting fine needles into specific points on the body, called acupoints, to stimulate energy flow, or "Qi" (pronounced "chee"). For animals, just as for humans, the Qi must flow freely for the body to function properly. When this flow is disrupted—whether due to illness, injury, or emotional stress—imbalances occur, leading to pain or other symptoms. Acupuncture seeks to restore the natural flow of Qi, promoting healing and reducing discomfort. It has been found particularly effective in treating conditions like arthritis, musculoskeletal issues, digestive disorders, and chronic pain in pets.

The energetic foundation of acupuncture lies in the idea that the body has invisible pathways known as meridians through which energy flows. When energy becomes blocked in these meridians, disease or discomfort results. Acupuncture works by unblocking these pathways, allowing the body's energy to flow freely once more, and facilitating natural healing. While acupuncture may sound invasive, it is actually a gentle and calming therapy for most animals. In fact, many pets become visibly relaxed during acupuncture sessions, showing how effectively it can help to calm and rebalance their energy.

Aromatherapy is another powerful holistic practice, one that taps into the sense of smell to influence the brain and nervous system of animals. Essential oils, which are concentrated extracts from plants, contain active compounds that can have a variety of effects on a pet's mood and health. Lavender oil, for instance, is known for its calming properties, helping to reduce stress and anxiety in pets. On the other hand, oils like peppermint or rosemary can be stimulating, helping to invigorate a pet's energy and alleviate fatigue. Aromatherapy can be particularly helpful in managing stress, separation anxiety, or hyperactivity in pets.

One key aspect of aromatherapy is understanding how different essential oils affect the animal's energetic body. Each scent resonates at a particular frequency and can influence the energy centers, or chakras, of the animal. For example, rose oil, with its gentle, loving energy, is often used to help balance the heart chakra, promoting emotional healing and comfort. Pet owners must be cautious, however, to use only pet-safe essential oils, as some oils, such as tea tree oil, can be toxic to certain animals. Proper dilution of oils is also crucial, as animals have a much more sensitive sense of smell than humans.

In addition to applying oils topically (when appropriately diluted), another popular method is diffusing them into the air, creating a calming or energizing atmosphere for the pet. Aromatherapy can be easily integrated into a pet's daily routine by using a diffuser in their living space or adding a few drops of essential oils to their bedding. This practice not only helps with physical ailments but can also balance emotional and mental states, encouraging a harmonious living environment for both pets and their owners.

Chromotherapy, or color therapy, is a lesser-known but equally powerful holistic modality that uses color to influence an animal's energy. Each color has a specific vibration and frequency that corresponds to different aspects of physical, mental, and emotional health. Red, for example, is energizing and can be used to stimulate circulation or increase vitality in sluggish or lethargic pets. On the opposite end of the spectrum, blue is calming and soothing, making it ideal for reducing stress and anxiety or helping to manage pain and inflammation.

The principles of chromotherapy can be applied in various ways. One common method is to bathe a room or space in colored light, using special lamps or light filters to create a healing environment for the pet. Another approach involves incorporating colored objects—such as blankets, toys, or bowls—into the pet's space, subtly influencing their energy throughout the day. Pet owners can even use colored crystals as part of the healing process, placing them around the animal's bed or living area to enhance the effects of chromotherapy. For example, placing a red crystal near a lethargic pet can help boost their energy, while a green crystal might be used to promote healing from illness or injury.

Reiki is another key modality in holistic pet care, one that focuses on channeling universal energy to promote healing and balance. Originally developed in Japan, Reiki works on the principle that a trained practitioner can transfer healing energy through their hands to the pet. This energy flows into the pet's body, restoring balance and removing blockages in their energy field. Reiki is a gentle, non-invasive therapy that can be performed hands-on, by placing hands directly on the animal's body, or even hands-off, through distance healing, making it a versatile option for all types of pets.

The core of Reiki is the belief that all living beings are surrounded by an energy field, or aura, which can become weakened or imbalanced due to stress, illness, or trauma. Reiki practitioners work to clear and strengthen this energy field, encouraging the pet's body to heal itself naturally. This practice is particularly helpful for animals recovering from surgery, dealing with chronic conditions, or experiencing emotional trauma, such as those who have been abused or neglected. Many pet owners find that Reiki helps to improve their pet's overall mood and behavior, as well as supporting physical healing.

One of the key benefits of Reiki is its ability to create a calm and safe environment for pets. Because it works on an energetic level, Reiki does not require physical contact, which is ideal for pets who may be shy, anxious, or uncomfortable with being touched. Reiki can also be used alongside other holistic treatments, such as massage or aromatherapy, to enhance their effects. When a pet is in a relaxed, open state, healing can take place more efficiently, making Reiki a valuable tool in any holistic care regimen.

Regardless of the modality chosen, one of the most important aspects of holistic treatments is the environment in which they are performed. Animals, being highly sensitive to energy, respond best when they feel safe, secure, and calm. Before starting any treatment, it is essential to create a serene and stress-free atmosphere for the pet. This might involve playing calming music, using essential oils in a diffuser, or simply ensuring that the pet's space is free from loud noises or sudden disruptions.

A peaceful environment helps the pet to relax, making them more receptive to healing. For many pets, the process of receiving holistic treatments can be deeply soothing, offering not only physical relief but also emotional and mental rejuvenation. The bond between pet and owner plays a crucial role here; the more relaxed and confident the owner is during the treatment, the more likely the pet will feel comfortable and open to receiving healing.

Holistic care empowers pet owners to take a proactive role in their pet's well-being. By learning and applying these therapies, owners can support their pets through physical ailments, emotional challenges, and behavioral issues, fostering a deeper connection and a more balanced, harmonious life for their beloved companions. Whether through acupuncture, aromatherapy, chromotherapy, or Reiki, holistic treatments provide a pathway to enhanced vitality and longevity, promoting health in its most complete and integrated form.

Chapter 2
Vital Energy and the Connection with Animals

Vital energy, often referred to as "life force" or "Qi" in some traditions, is a fundamental concept in holistic healing. This energy flows through all living beings, including animals, and is considered essential for maintaining health and balance. In holistic pet care, understanding how this energy works, how it interacts with the body, and how it affects an animal's overall well-being is crucial. Vital energy influences everything from physical health to emotional states and behavior, and disruptions or imbalances in this energy can manifest as illness, stress, or behavioral problems in animals.

The flow of vital energy in animals follows specific patterns within their bodies, much like it does in humans. In traditional Chinese medicine, this energy flows through channels or meridians, connecting various organs and systems. These meridians ensure that energy reaches every part of the body, maintaining health and vitality. When energy flows smoothly, an animal feels healthy, active, and balanced. However, blockages, deficiencies, or excesses of energy in these pathways can lead to problems, ranging from minor discomforts like restlessness or anxiety to more severe physical conditions such as chronic pain or digestive issues.

One of the most profound ways vital energy expresses itself in animals is through their behavior and emotional responses. Animals, especially those closely bonded with humans, are highly intuitive and sensitive to the energies around them. Changes in their environment, stress from their owners, or even shifts in household dynamics can affect their energy balance. An energetic connection between a pet and its human companion is powerful and should be nurtured as part of their overall health.

Animals often act as mirrors of the energies around them, including the energy of their environment and their owners. For example, a dog living in a high-stress household may begin to show signs of anxiety or nervousness, reflecting the energetic state of its human companions. Conversely, when the animal's own energy is balanced, they tend to exhibit calmness, confidence, and overall health. Thus, in many ways, pets serve as barometers for the energy in their environment, responding to subtle shifts that humans may not even be aware of.

A key aspect of vital energy in animals is the presence of energy centers known as chakras. While chakra theory is often associated with human spirituality, animals also have chakras that govern different aspects of their physical and emotional well-being. These energy centers are responsible for regulating the flow of vital energy within the body, influencing everything from physical health to emotional balance. When the chakras are in balance, energy flows freely, and the animal remains healthy and content. When they are blocked or out of balance, the animal may experience various forms of distress, such as physical illness, anxiety, or behavioral problems.

The chakra system in animals is similar to that of humans, with seven main chakras aligned along the spine, each associated with specific physical, emotional, and energetic functions. Starting at the base of the spine is the Root Chakra, which governs physical survival, security, and grounding. This chakra is connected to an animal's sense of safety and stability in its environment. When the Root Chakra is balanced, the pet feels secure, calm, and grounded. Imbalances in this chakra can lead to issues like fearfulness, aggression, or excessive nervousness.

Moving upwards, the Sacral Chakra, located just below the belly, is associated with emotions, creativity, and reproduction. In pets, this chakra influences their emotional behavior, including how they interact with other animals and humans. A balanced Sacral Chakra results in a happy, well-adjusted pet, while imbalances can manifest as mood swings, anxiety, or reproductive issues. This chakra is especially important in animals who have experienced trauma or emotional distress, as it can hold onto emotional energy that needs to be released.

The Solar Plexus Chakra, located near the stomach, is responsible for personal power, confidence, and self-esteem. In animals, this chakra influences their sense of control and their confidence in the world around them. A dog with a balanced Solar Plexus Chakra, for instance, will exhibit confidence in its interactions with other animals and people. On the other hand, an imbalance in this chakra might result in timid or overly aggressive behavior. This energy center is crucial for pets who struggle with fear or dominance issues, as restoring balance here can help them regain their natural confidence.

The Heart Chakra, located at the center of the chest, governs love, compassion, and emotional connection. This chakra is vital for forming bonds with others, whether with humans or other animals. A pet with a healthy, open Heart Chakra will be affectionate, loving, and connected to its family. Imbalances in the Heart Chakra may result in behavioral issues such as withdrawal, fear of relationships, or excessive clinginess. Pets who have been abandoned, neglected, or abused often have blockages in their Heart Chakra that require healing to restore their emotional balance.

Moving up to the Throat Chakra, located at the base of the throat, this energy center governs communication and self-expression. In pets, this chakra influences their ability to express their needs, desires, and emotions. For example, a cat that has trouble vocalizing or a dog that seems withdrawn may have a blocked Throat Chakra. When this chakra is balanced, the pet can express itself clearly and appropriately, whether through vocalizations or other forms of communication. Imbalances can lead to issues with excessive barking, difficulty in communicating needs, or even physical issues related to the throat or neck area.

The Third Eye Chakra, located between the eyes, is connected to intuition, perception, and insight. This chakra allows animals to sense the world around them beyond just physical senses, tapping into their instincts and deeper understanding. Animals, by nature, are highly intuitive beings, and this chakra plays a crucial role in their ability to sense changes in their environment or in the emotional states of those around them. When the Third Eye Chakra is balanced, animals display heightened awareness and understanding. Imbalances can lead to confusion, disorientation, or behavioral issues that seem out of character for the pet.

At the crown of the head lies the Crown Chakra, which governs spiritual connection and awareness. This chakra connects animals to the larger world, including the energies of nature, other beings, and even their human companions. A balanced Crown Chakra helps an animal feel at peace and aligned with the world around them, promoting a sense of calm and well-being. Imbalances in this chakra may cause restlessness or a sense of disconnection from their surroundings or their owners.

The concept of vital energy and the chakra system provides a framework for understanding how holistic treatments can influence an animal's well-being. By working to balance the flow of energy in the body and clear blockages in the chakras, pet owners can help their animals maintain a state of harmony and health. This approach can be especially beneficial for pets with chronic health issues, behavioral problems, or emotional trauma, as it addresses not just the symptoms but the underlying energetic causes of distress.

Understanding the flow of vital energy and its connection to an animal's health allows for more targeted, effective holistic care. Whether through energy healing techniques, like Reiki, or physical treatments, like acupuncture and massage, the goal is to restore balance and promote natural healing from within. When energy flows freely and the chakras are balanced, pets are not only healthier but also happier and more content, enhancing their quality of life in every way.

Building upon the understanding of vital energy and its significance in maintaining the well-being of animals, we now turn to methods for assessing and restoring the balance of this energy. Holistic therapies often rely on the ability to recognize when an animal's energy is disrupted or blocked, and knowing how to gently guide this energy back into harmony is key to effective treatment. This chapter will explore practical techniques to assess the flow of energy in animals and simple yet powerful methods for restoring balance, such as breathing exercises, visualization, and energy work.

The first step in addressing any energetic imbalance in an animal is learning to identify the signs of disrupted energy flow. Since animals cannot verbally communicate discomfort in the same way humans do, it is essential to observe their behavior, physical condition, and even their emotional responses. Changes in an animal's demeanor—such as increased anxiety, aggression, or withdrawal—can be indicative of energy blockages. Likewise, physical symptoms such as stiffness, digestive issues, or skin problems may suggest that energy is not flowing properly through certain parts of the body.

Energetic blockages often manifest as specific physical issues in areas of the body that correspond to the chakras. For example, a blockage in the Root Chakra might result in symptoms related to the legs, lower back, or digestive system, as this chakra governs the animal's sense of stability and grounding. A blockage in the Heart Chakra, which governs emotions and the circulatory system, may manifest as lethargy, a lack of enthusiasm for play or interaction, or even cardiovascular issues. Recognizing these connections between physical symptoms and the animal's energy centers is crucial for assessing where blockages may be occurring.

In addition to behavioral and physical cues, pet owners can use intuitive observation to assess their pet's energy. Animals are extremely sensitive to touch, and by gently placing your hands on different areas of the pet's body, you can often sense where energy is stagnant or overactive. A healthy energy flow will feel warm, fluid, and even, whereas blockages may feel like coolness, tension, or uneven energy patterns. Practitioners of energy healing techniques, such as Reiki, often describe feeling changes in temperature or subtle vibrations when they encounter areas of energetic imbalance in the body.

Once an imbalance has been identified, the next step is to begin restoring the flow of energy. One of the most accessible and effective techniques for calming and balancing an animal's energy is the use of breathing exercises. Just as in humans, breath is a powerful tool for regulating energy in animals. Breathing exercises not only help to calm an anxious pet but also assist in releasing pent-up energy and restoring balance to the body's energy centers.

A simple breathing technique that can be used with pets involves synchronized breathing between the pet and the owner. To practice this, sit quietly with your pet in a calm, quiet space. Place one hand gently on the pet's chest or back, depending on where they seem comfortable, and begin to slow your own breathing. Inhale deeply and slowly, and then exhale gently. As you breathe, focus on feeling the rhythm of your pet's breathing and attempt to synchronize your breaths. This practice helps to calm the pet's nervous system, reduce anxiety, and bring their energy into harmony with yours. Over time, this exercise can deepen the bond between you and your pet while promoting overall energy balance.

Visualization techniques are another powerful tool for restoring energetic balance in animals. Visualization, combined with intention, can direct healing energy to specific areas of the pet's body or aura. This practice is especially effective when dealing with emotional imbalances or energy blockages in the chakras. To perform a visualization, begin by finding a quiet space where your pet feels safe and comfortable. Sit or stand close to your pet, allowing your energy to connect with theirs. Close your eyes and focus on your breathing, clearing your mind of distractions.

Once you are centered, begin to visualize a bright, healing light surrounding your pet. Imagine this light as a radiant glow that envelops their entire body, gently filling any areas of darkness or blockage with warmth and energy. You can visualize this light moving through your pet's body, flowing along the energy pathways and entering each chakra. As the light flows, imagine it dissolving any tension, pain, or emotional distress, leaving only a sense of calm and balance in its wake. Visualization exercises can be particularly effective for addressing specific chakras. For example, if your pet is struggling with anxiety, focus your visualization on the Solar Plexus Chakra, which governs confidence and emotional stability, or the Heart Chakra, which regulates emotional connections and love.

Another practical method for restoring balance to an animal's energy is light touch therapy. Similar to the principles of Reiki, light touch therapy involves placing the hands on or near the pet's body to channel healing energy into areas of need. This therapy is especially useful for calming stressed or anxious animals, as it promotes relaxation and encourages the natural flow of energy through the body. Begin by gently placing your hands on the pet's shoulders or back, where most animals feel safe and comfortable. Let your hands rest there, remaining still and calm. As you connect with your pet's energy, you may begin to sense areas where the energy feels "stuck" or stagnant.

In these areas, apply gentle pressure or move your hands slowly in circular motions to encourage the energy to flow again. It is essential to remain relaxed and patient during this process, as animals are highly sensitive to your emotional state. If you stay calm and focused, your pet will be more likely to respond positively to the treatment. Over time, light touch therapy can help dissolve energetic blockages and restore balance, especially when combined with other holistic practices such as breathing exercises or visualization.

Restoring an animal's energy balance can also be achieved through the use of energy-focused tools, such as crystals or healing stones. Crystals have long been used in holistic healing for their ability to store, transmit, and amplify energy. In animal therapy, specific crystals can be placed on or near the pet's body to target different chakras and promote energetic balance. For example, amethyst is known for its calming properties and can be used to soothe anxiety or emotional distress, while citrine is associated with energizing the Solar Plexus Chakra and boosting confidence and vitality.

To use crystals in an energy healing session, place the stones in the areas corresponding to the pet's chakras or near the parts of the body where energy blockages have been identified. Allow the pet to relax in a calm environment, and let the crystals do their work by emitting their natural vibrations into the pet's energy field. Crystals can also be placed around the pet's living space or near their bed to maintain a balanced energetic environment on a daily basis.

One additional method for clearing and balancing an animal's energy is through sound healing. Certain sounds and frequencies have been shown to influence energy flow, promoting relaxation and healing. Tibetan singing bowls, chimes, or even soothing music can be used during energy healing sessions to help dissolve blockages and calm the pet's mind and body. Sound therapy is especially useful for pets that are particularly sensitive to touch or handling, as the vibrations of sound can penetrate deep into the body and aura without the need for physical contact.

The ultimate goal of these holistic techniques is to restore a free and balanced flow of vital energy in the animal's body, allowing their natural healing processes to take over. When energy flows smoothly, the pet is more likely to experience good health, emotional stability, and a deeper sense of connection with their environment and their human companions. These practices, whether performed individually or in combination, offer powerful tools for pet owners to support their animals' well-being on a holistic and energetic level.

Through consistent practice and mindful observation, pet owners can develop a deeper understanding of their pets' energetic needs, allowing them to respond more effectively to imbalances and promote long-term health and harmony. The connection between animals and their vital energy is profound, and by learning to work with this energy, we can help ensure that our pets thrive in body, mind, and spirit.

Chapter 3
Massage Techniques to Calm and Revitalize

Massage therapy, a well-established practice in human health, has gained popularity as a valuable holistic treatment for pets. It offers not only physical benefits, such as relieving muscle tension and improving circulation, but also profound emotional and energetic advantages. Through touch, massage can help calm anxious animals, reduce stress, and promote overall well-being. For pets, the experience of therapeutic massage is often both soothing and revitalizing, strengthening their bond with their human companions and promoting trust and comfort.

The power of massage lies in its ability to connect deeply with the animal's body and energy field. When performed mindfully, massage techniques can help release physical tension and energetic blockages, restoring balance to the body. This chapter introduces simple massage techniques designed to calm and revitalize pets, emphasizing how these practices can be integrated into daily routines for stress relief and improved physical health.

One of the first and most important benefits of massage is relaxation. For many pets, especially those who experience anxiety, stress, or nervousness, gentle touch can provide an immediate sense of security. Animals, like humans, hold stress in their muscles and tissues. This tension can lead to stiffness, discomfort, and even behavioral issues over time. Regular massage helps release this built-up tension, allowing the animal to relax and feel more at ease in its body and environment. It also encourages the release of endorphins, the body's natural "feel-good" chemicals, which help to elevate mood and promote a sense of calm.

To begin a massage session with your pet, it's essential to create a calm, quiet environment where the animal feels safe. Choose a space where there are minimal distractions, and use soft lighting or calming sounds to enhance the relaxation process. Before starting, ensure your pet is comfortable and willing to participate. Unlike humans, animals can't verbally express their discomfort, so it's important to read their body language. Signs of relaxation include soft eyes, relaxed ears, and a loose, comfortable posture. If the pet shows signs of discomfort or anxiety—such as pulling away, growling, or tensing—pause and reassess the situation before proceeding.

The most basic technique to begin with is a gentle, full-body stroking motion, which helps relax the muscles and prepares the pet for more targeted massage techniques. Start at the top of the head and move slowly down the spine, applying light, even pressure with your hands. Use long, smooth strokes to cover larger muscle groups, such as the shoulders, back, and hindquarters. This helps to warm the muscles and distribute energy throughout the body. Be sure to keep your touch soft and steady, as animals are highly sensitive to changes in pressure. If your pet seems to enjoy the stroking, you can gradually increase the firmness of your touch to provide deeper relaxation.

Next, focus on key areas where pets often hold tension, particularly around the neck, shoulders, and back. The neck and shoulder area is especially prone to tightness in dogs and cats, as they often carry stress in these regions. To release tension here, use your fingertips to apply light circular motions at the base of the neck and along the top of the shoulders. These small, gentle circles help to break up tight knots in the muscles and encourage relaxation. As you work through these areas, observe your pet's responses—if they lean into your touch or show signs of enjoyment, you're on the right track. If they seem tense or resistant, lighten your pressure and proceed more slowly.

Massaging the back is another key area for pets, as it houses many large muscle groups that can become stiff or sore from daily activity. To massage the back, place both hands on either side of the spine and apply light, downward pressure as you move from the neck to the base of the tail. Avoid pressing directly on the spine itself, as this can be uncomfortable or even harmful. Instead, focus on the muscles along the sides of the spine, using your thumbs to apply gentle pressure in circular motions. This helps to increase blood flow, loosen tight muscles, and stimulate the flow of vital energy along the pet's back.

As you continue the massage, don't forget the legs and paws. Many pets, especially older animals, experience joint stiffness and discomfort in their legs, which can benefit greatly from gentle massage. Start by gently stroking the legs to relax the muscles, then apply light pressure with your fingers along the length of each leg, using a kneading motion. Be particularly gentle around the joints—knees, elbows, and hips—where pets are most likely to experience discomfort. For the paws, use your thumbs to apply gentle pressure to the pads, moving in slow, circular motions. Paws are sensitive areas for many animals, so proceed cautiously and observe how your pet responds.

Massage is not only a physical treatment but also a way to engage with the pet's energy field. As you massage, pay attention to the energy flow in your pet's body. Are there areas that feel tense or blocked, where the energy seems to "stick"? Are there areas that feel warm or calm, where energy flows smoothly? By attuning yourself to your pet's energetic responses, you can begin to identify where blockages may exist and tailor your massage to help release them. For example, if you notice tension around the heart area, you might focus more attention on massaging the chest and upper back to promote the flow of energy through the Heart Chakra.

One of the most profound benefits of massage is the deepening of the bond between pet and owner. Touch is one of the primary ways animals communicate affection and trust, and by engaging in regular massage sessions, you create a space where your pet feels loved, cared for, and secure. This can be especially important for rescue animals or pets that have experienced trauma or neglect, as they may be more wary of physical contact. Through gentle, positive touch, you can help rebuild their trust in humans and foster a stronger emotional connection.

For animals with anxiety, massage can serve as a powerful tool for calming the nervous system. By working on key acupressure points, such as those located on the ears or along the spine, you can help stimulate the parasympathetic nervous system, which is responsible for relaxation and healing. To perform an ear massage, use your fingertips to gently rub the base of the ears, moving in small, circular motions. The ears are home to several acupressure points that can help release tension and promote relaxation. This technique is particularly useful for pets that become anxious during thunderstorms, fireworks, or other stressful situations.

In addition to promoting relaxation, massage can also play a role in revitalizing an animal's energy. By stimulating circulation and encouraging the flow of energy through the body, massage helps to rejuvenate tired or sluggish pets, making it an ideal practice for older animals or those recovering from illness or injury. After a massage, many pets display increased energy and enthusiasm, as their bodies feel more aligned and free from tension. In this way, massage serves as both a calming and energizing treatment, depending on the needs of the individual animal.

It is important to remember that massage should always be a gentle, positive experience for the pet. The goal is not to force the animal into a state of relaxation but to create a space where they can naturally release tension and stress. As you practice massage, tune into your pet's needs and responses, adjusting your techniques as necessary. Each animal is unique, and what works for one pet may not be effective for another. Over time, you'll develop a deeper understanding of your pet's preferences and how to use massage to enhance their well-being.

Massage therapy for pets is a versatile and effective holistic treatment that not only promotes physical health but also fosters emotional balance and strengthens the human-animal bond. By incorporating simple massage techniques into your pet's routine, you can help relieve stress, improve circulation, and support the natural flow of energy through their body. Whether your pet is anxious, aging, or simply in need of a calming touch, massage offers a gentle and powerful way to enhance their quality of life, bringing peace and vitality into their everyday experience.

As we continue exploring the art of therapeutic massage for pets, we will delve into more advanced techniques aimed at addressing chronic pain, improving circulation, and revitalizing your pet's energy centers. Beyond the foundational strokes and calming methods introduced in the previous chapter, these advanced practices can help unblock specific energy points and deepen the connection between pet and owner. By learning how to work with your pet's body more precisely, you can tailor your massages to meet their individual needs, whether they suffer from chronic conditions, mobility issues, or simply need revitalization.

One of the key goals of advanced massage techniques is to address chronic pain, which can be a common issue for aging pets or those with conditions like arthritis, hip dysplasia, or muscle injuries. Massage, when performed with care and attention, can help alleviate the discomfort associated with these conditions by improving blood circulation, reducing muscle stiffness, and promoting the natural release of endorphins—the body's natural pain relievers. In this way, massage becomes an essential part of a holistic healing regimen, complementing veterinary care and other therapies.

A technique particularly beneficial for managing chronic pain is trigger point therapy. Trigger points, or "knots," are areas of the muscle that have become tense and painful due to stress, overuse, or injury. These areas can cause discomfort not only in the immediate region but can also refer pain to other parts of the body. For example, a trigger point in the lower back muscles can contribute to stiffness or pain in the legs. To help relieve these painful points, you can use focused pressure applied with your thumb or fingertips.

To perform trigger point therapy, start by gently palpating the muscles around the affected area. You may notice small, tender knots or bands of tension—these are the trigger points. Once you identify them, apply light, steady pressure with your thumb or fingertips, holding the pressure for 10 to 30 seconds before releasing. As you apply pressure, you may feel the muscle begin to soften or relax under your touch. It's important to proceed slowly and mindfully, as applying too much pressure too quickly can cause discomfort. Trigger point therapy should be done gradually, with sessions spaced out to allow the muscles to heal and release tension over time.

In addition to trigger point therapy, another advanced technique for alleviating pain and revitalizing energy is cross-fiber friction. This method involves applying firm, transverse (crosswise) strokes across the muscle fibers rather than along their length. Cross-fiber friction helps break up adhesions or scar tissue that may have formed as a result of injury or chronic tension. This technique can be especially useful for pets recovering from injuries, as it helps promote flexibility and mobility in the muscles and joints.

To perform cross-fiber friction, use your fingertips or thumb to apply firm, small strokes perpendicular to the muscle fibers. For example, if you're working on a pet's shoulder, where the muscle fibers run lengthwise along the body, you would move your thumb horizontally across the fibers. This motion helps increase blood flow to the area, promoting healing and reducing stiffness. As with any massage technique, be mindful of your pet's responses, adjusting the pressure and intensity as needed to keep them comfortable.

Along with relieving pain, massage is also highly effective in improving circulation, which is crucial for maintaining the health of all bodily systems. Improved circulation helps oxygenate tissues, remove metabolic waste products, and promote lymphatic drainage, all of which contribute to the overall health and vitality of your pet. For pets with mobility issues or those who spend a lot of time lying down, massage can help prevent issues like poor circulation, muscle atrophy, or the buildup of toxins in the tissues.

To enhance circulation through massage, focus on techniques that promote the flow of blood and lymph through the body. One such technique is effleurage, a series of long, sweeping strokes that move fluid through the tissues and stimulate the lymphatic system. To perform effleurage, use both hands to apply light pressure, beginning at the extremities (such as the paws or legs) and moving toward the heart. For example, when massaging the legs, start at the paws and use smooth, rhythmic strokes to move up toward the hip or shoulder. This helps encourage the natural flow of lymph, which is essential for detoxification and immune system function.

Another way to revitalize your pet's body through massage is to work with the animal's chakras and energy points. As discussed in previous chapters, animals have energy centers, or chakras, that correspond to different physical, emotional, and energetic aspects of their being. By integrating chakra balancing techniques into your massage sessions, you can enhance the flow of energy through these centers, helping to clear blockages and restore vitality to the body.

To balance the chakras through massage, you can apply gentle, circular motions over the areas where the chakras are located. For example, the Root Chakra is located at the base of the spine, and gently massaging this area can help promote feelings of grounding and security. Similarly, massaging the chest area where the Heart Chakra resides can help release emotional tension and foster a deeper connection between you and your pet. The Solar Plexus Chakra, which governs confidence and energy, can be revitalized by massaging the stomach area in slow, clockwise circles.

As you work with the chakras, visualize healing energy flowing through your hands and into your pet's body. This intention can help guide your touch and deepen the energetic effects of the massage. In addition to physical touch, you can incorporate crystals, essential oils, or healing music into the session to further enhance the chakra balancing process. For instance, placing a rose quartz crystal near your pet's chest during a massage can help amplify the healing energy of the Heart Chakra, while playing calming music can create a soothing atmosphere that supports the overall healing experience.

One often overlooked area of massage is the head and face, which can have a profound impact on your pet's relaxation and emotional balance. Many animals, especially those prone to stress or anxiety, hold a significant amount of tension in the muscles around the face, jaw, and ears. By incorporating gentle head and face massage techniques into your routine, you can help your pet release this tension and experience a deeper sense of calm.

To massage the head and face, start by gently rubbing the top of the head and the base of the ears in slow, circular motions. Many pets find ear massages particularly soothing, as this area contains acupressure points that help relax the nervous system. After massaging the ears, move down to the jawline, where tension often accumulates. Use your fingertips to apply light pressure along the jaw, moving from the back of the jaw toward the chin. This helps release tightness in the jaw muscles, which can be especially beneficial for dogs or cats that chew on hard objects or are prone to clenching their teeth.

When massaging the face, be gentle and mindful of your pet's comfort, as this is a sensitive area. Always watch for signs that your pet is enjoying the massage—softened facial expressions, relaxed body posture, or even a contented sigh are good indicators that the techniques are working. On the other hand, if your pet pulls away or shows signs of discomfort, stop the massage and give them space to relax before continuing.

Advanced massage techniques also provide an opportunity to deepen the bond between pet and owner. Massage requires focus, patience, and attunement to your pet's needs, and through this process, you become more in tune with their body language and energy. This heightened awareness fosters a greater sense of trust and connection, as your pet learns to associate your touch with feelings of comfort and safety. Over time, regular massage can become a cherished part of your daily routine, providing both physical and emotional benefits for your pet.

Finally, it's important to integrate massage into a broader holistic healing regimen. While massage is a powerful tool for promoting health and well-being, it works best when combined with other holistic practices such as proper nutrition, exercise, and energy work. Ensuring that your pet's diet is balanced, providing them with mental stimulation and regular physical activity, and using complementary therapies like aromatherapy or Reiki can enhance the effects of massage and contribute to your pet's overall vitality.

In conclusion, advanced massage techniques offer a versatile and effective way to address chronic pain, improve circulation, and revitalize your pet's energy centers. Whether your pet is suffering from stiffness, recovering from injury, or simply needs relaxation, these techniques can be tailored to meet their individual needs. By incorporating trigger point therapy, cross-fiber friction, chakra balancing, and head and face massages into your routine, you can provide deeper, more targeted care that enhances both the physical and energetic well-being of your beloved companion.

Chapter 4
Aromatherapy
Using Essential Oils for Pet Well-Being

Aromatherapy, the therapeutic use of essential oils, has long been valued for its ability to influence both mental and physical health. In the context of pet care, it offers a gentle and effective way to enhance well-being, relieve anxiety, and support healing processes. Essential oils, derived from plants, are highly concentrated and contain the essence of the plant's natural healing properties. They can be used to calm an anxious animal, stimulate an energetic one, or even address physical ailments like inflammation or skin conditions.

It's important to understand that while many essential oils can be beneficial to pets, not all are safe for use. Animals, especially cats, have a heightened sensitivity to many substances, including essential oils. Therefore, choosing the right oils and using them correctly is critical to ensuring the well-being of your pet. For instance, oils like lavender, chamomile, and frankincense are commonly used in pet aromatherapy due to their calming and healing properties. On the other hand, oils such as tea tree, cinnamon, and citrus can be toxic, particularly to cats, and should be avoided.

The key to using aromatherapy effectively with pets is ensuring that the oils are diluted properly. Because animals have a more sensitive sense of smell than humans, essential oils should never be used in their pure, undiluted form. Diluting oils with a carrier oil—such as coconut oil, almond oil, or olive oil—not only makes them safer for pets but also helps to spread the oil more evenly when applying it topically. A typical dilution for animals is much lower than for humans; for most pets, a dilution of 1-2 drops of essential oil in a tablespoon of carrier oil is sufficient.

There are several ways to introduce essential oils into your pet's environment, each method offering its own benefits. One of the most common and effective methods is diffusion. By using a diffuser, you can disperse the essential oil into the air in small, controlled amounts. This is especially helpful for animals who may be nervous or anxious, as the aroma can fill the space and provide a calming effect without directly applying the oil to the pet. For example, diffusing lavender oil in a room where your dog rests can create a soothing atmosphere, helping to reduce stress during thunderstorms or other anxiety-inducing events.

Topical application is another way to use essential oils for pet well-being, although this method requires careful consideration. Some pets, especially dogs, tolerate topical application better than others, and it's always advisable to perform a patch test on a small area of the skin before applying oils more widely. Once diluted, oils like chamomile can be massaged into sore muscles to ease tension or applied to dry, irritated skin to promote healing. When applying essential oils to your pet, avoid sensitive areas such as the eyes, nose, and genitals. It's also important to ensure that your pet doesn't lick the area where the oil has been applied, as ingestion can lead to stomach upset or other adverse reactions.

Inhalation is another method that works well for aromatherapy, particularly when the goal is to reduce stress or calm an anxious animal. This method can be as simple as allowing your pet to smell a cotton ball or cloth infused with a few drops of diluted essential oil. For example, if your pet is nervous before a trip to the vet, you can let them inhale a bit of lavender or frankincense from a cloth before the journey, helping to calm their nerves and ease tension.

Certain essential oils are known to have specific effects on an animal's nervous system, making them particularly useful for addressing behavioral or emotional challenges. Lavender, one of the most popular oils in aromatherapy, is renowned for its calming properties. It can help reduce stress, ease anxiety, and promote restful sleep, making it ideal for pets who are nervous or have trouble relaxing. Roman chamomile is another excellent choice for its ability to soothe irritation and promote calmness, especially in high-strung animals.

Frankincense, on the other hand, has grounding and balancing properties, making it useful for pets who are recovering from trauma or dealing with emotional imbalances. It helps strengthen the immune system and encourages a sense of security and stability. Peppermint, while generally stimulating, can also help soothe digestive issues when used appropriately, although it should be used sparingly and avoided with very young or sensitive animals.

Aromatherapy is not only about using oils to address specific issues but also about creating a peaceful and healing environment for your pet. For example, if you're creating a calm space where your pet can retreat to relax, incorporating soothing scents like lavender or chamomile through a diffuser can enhance the space's energy, encouraging your pet to unwind. Similarly, if your pet is recovering from illness or injury, using uplifting and revitalizing oils like rosemary or peppermint in the environment can help boost their mood and energy levels as they heal.

It's also important to note the emotional connection that scents can create between pet and owner. Animals are highly attuned to their environment and the energies of their human companions, and the use of certain scents can strengthen this bond. When a pet associates a particular scent with positive experiences—such as a relaxing massage or a calm atmosphere—they may begin to associate that scent with feelings of safety and comfort. Over time, using the same essential oils during calming routines can signal to the pet that it's time to relax, reinforcing their sense of security.

Before beginning any aromatherapy regimen for your pet, it's essential to consult with a veterinarian, especially one experienced in holistic treatments. They can guide you on the best practices for using essential oils safely and effectively, based on your pet's specific health needs, sensitivities, and breed characteristics. Additionally, it's crucial to monitor your pet's reactions to aromatherapy closely. Signs that an essential oil may not be well-tolerated include excessive drooling, coughing, sneezing, or rubbing the face or body. If your pet shows any signs of discomfort, stop using the oil immediately and consult a professional.

Incorporating aromatherapy into your pet's wellness routine can be a gentle yet powerful way to support their physical and emotional health. Whether you're helping a nervous pet relax, easing muscle soreness, or simply creating a peaceful environment, essential oils offer a wide range of benefits when used with care and intention. By understanding the principles of aromatherapy and selecting the right oils for your pet's unique needs, you can enhance their well-being in a holistic and natural way, deepening your connection with them through the healing power of scent.

As we move into more advanced applications of aromatherapy for pets, this chapter explores how to combine essential oils for specific purposes, such as treating anxiety, relieving pain, or boosting vitality. Blending oils allows for a more customized approach to your pet's health, targeting multiple needs at once. We will also discuss different techniques for administering aromatherapy beyond basic diffusion and topical applications, including how to use oil blends in a more integrated way through massage, baths, and energy work.

Creating custom blends of essential oils offers the opportunity to address multiple issues in your pet's life, whether they are emotional, physical, or energetic in nature. For example, a pet suffering from both anxiety and muscle pain might benefit from a blend of lavender for its calming effects and marjoram for its muscle-relaxing properties. When blending oils, it's essential to keep the individual oils' properties in mind and how they might interact with each other. Start with a primary oil that addresses the main issue and then add one or two supporting oils that complement its effects.

Blending essential oils not only enhances their therapeutic effects but also helps to create a more complex and enjoyable aroma, which is important for maintaining your pet's comfort and well-being. For example, if your dog tends to get anxious during thunderstorms, a blend of lavender, Roman chamomile, and cedarwood can create a soothing atmosphere that reduces stress and promotes relaxation. Cedarwood, in particular, has grounding properties that can help animals feel more secure, while chamomile amplifies the calming effects of lavender.

Another effective blend for pets with chronic pain or inflammation might include frankincense, which has anti-inflammatory properties, combined with ginger or turmeric oils, known for their ability to ease pain and promote circulation. Adding a drop of peppermint can enhance this blend, as its cooling sensation soothes aches and pains, though it's important to use peppermint in very small amounts and ensure it's well-diluted, as it can be too strong for sensitive animals.

Once you have created a blend, there are several ways to administer it. In addition to using a diffuser, you can incorporate essential oils into massage sessions. Applying a diluted blend to your hands and gently massaging it into the pet's muscles allows the oils to absorb into the skin while promoting relaxation and circulation through touch. This method is particularly beneficial for animals suffering from chronic conditions such as arthritis or hip dysplasia, where both the massage and the oil work in tandem to relieve pain and stiffness.

Another method to apply essential oil blends is through bathing. Adding a few drops of a diluted essential oil blend to your pet's bath water can provide both a physical and aromatic benefit. Oils like lavender and chamomile work wonderfully in bath water for soothing irritated skin, while a blend of rosemary and eucalyptus can help refresh and invigorate. However, be cautious when using oils in the bath, as some animals may try to drink the water, so always monitor them closely during this process.

Inhalation techniques, such as steaming, can also be useful, particularly for pets with respiratory issues. To create an aromatic steam, place a few drops of essential oil into a bowl of hot water and allow your pet to sit nearby, inhaling the vapors. This method is highly effective for clearing congestion or soothing irritated airways, especially when using oils like eucalyptus or frankincense. Be careful to ensure your pet does not get too close to the hot water, or breathe in too much of the vapors at once, as this can be overwhelming for their sensitive respiratory system. It's always best to create a gentle, indirect exposure to the steam and to monitor your pet closely for any signs of discomfort.

When using aromatherapy to treat anxiety, a common issue for many pets, it's important to choose oils that not only calm the animal but also address the specific triggers of their anxiety. For example, separation anxiety can be effectively managed with a blend of lavender, vetiver, and cedarwood. Lavender, as previously mentioned, helps with relaxation, while vetiver is known for its deeply grounding properties, helping pets feel more secure when their owners are away. Cedarwood, on the other hand, can provide a sense of warmth and safety. For pets with general anxiety triggered by loud noises, new environments, or travel, a similar blend may be used, with adjustments depending on the pet's individual reactions to each oil.

For application, consider rubbing a small amount of diluted oil blend onto your hands before interacting with your pet, especially if they are prone to anxiety in particular situations, like before a vet visit or a long car ride. This allows them to associate your scent with a calming presence. Alternatively, you can apply the diluted blend to a bandana or collar that the pet wears, allowing them to benefit from the oils throughout the day.

Aromatherapy can also be beneficial in revitalizing pets that suffer from lethargy, fatigue, or a general lack of energy. In these cases, stimulating and energizing oils, such as rosemary, peppermint, and lemongrass, can be helpful. Rosemary is known for its invigorating properties and can boost circulation, helping pets feel more alert and energized. Lemongrass, with its bright, citrusy scent, can refresh a tired pet and uplift their mood. Peppermint, although potent and requiring careful dilution, can stimulate both physical and mental activity, making it useful for older pets or those recovering from illness.

For pets who are recuperating from surgery or illness and need a gentle energy boost, consider using an essential oil blend that includes ginger, frankincense, and sweet orange. Ginger can help stimulate circulation and digestion, while frankincense supports overall healing and emotional balance. Sweet orange brings a gentle, uplifting energy without being overly stimulating, making it suitable for convalescing pets. This blend can be diffused in the room or applied topically (properly diluted) to areas where the pet needs support, such as near joints or sore muscles.

In addition to physical ailments, aromatherapy can play a role in addressing behavioral issues. Pets, like humans, can develop negative behavioral patterns due to stress, fear, or discomfort. By using essential oils that promote calmness, focus, or security, you can help shift these patterns and support healthier behaviors. For example, dogs that are prone to excessive barking or hyperactivity may benefit from calming oils like chamomile, vetiver, or sandalwood. These oils can help them settle down and feel less reactive to external stimuli.

On the other hand, cats that exhibit territorial behavior or aggression may respond well to oils like frankincense or cedarwood, which promote emotional balance and security. Since cats are particularly sensitive to essential oils, it's crucial to use a well-diluted mixture and avoid direct application. Instead, diffusing a calming blend in the space where your cat spends the most time can subtly influence their mood without overwhelming their senses.

Aromatherapy can also be integrated into energy healing practices such as Reiki or crystal therapy. Essential oils like lavender, frankincense, and sandalwood are often used during energy healing sessions to help open and balance the chakras. For example, applying a diluted lavender blend to the area of the pet's heart chakra before a Reiki session can help facilitate emotional release and enhance the healing energy flow. Likewise, using grounding oils like vetiver or cedarwood during a massage session focused on the root chakra can help stabilize the pet's energy and promote a sense of security.

Another powerful way to incorporate aromatherapy into your pet's holistic care routine is through environmental aromatherapy. This involves creating a healing atmosphere in your pet's living space by regularly diffusing calming or revitalizing essential oils. Whether your goal is to create a tranquil environment that reduces anxiety or to energize your pet during playtime, the strategic use of essential oils in the home can have lasting benefits on your pet's mood and overall well-being. For instance, diffusing chamomile or lavender in your pet's sleeping area can help improve their sleep quality, while oils like eucalyptus or peppermint can be used in common areas to keep energy levels high during the day.

It is also important to remember that some pets may be more sensitive to essential oils than others. This can depend on a variety of factors, including the species, age, size, and overall health of the animal. Always observe how your pet responds to a new oil, starting with very small amounts and gradually increasing exposure as you monitor their behavior. Signs of sensitivity or discomfort might include excessive sneezing, coughing, or avoidance of the area where the oil is being used. If any of these signs appear, stop using the oil immediately and consult your veterinarian.

As with any holistic treatment, consistency is key in aromatherapy. The benefits of essential oils are best observed over time, with regular, gentle exposure rather than intense or sporadic use. Incorporating essential oils into daily routines—whether during relaxation, playtime, or as part of a healing practice—allows your pet to become accustomed to the scents and their effects. Over time, you may notice improvements not only in their physical condition but also in their emotional and energetic balance.

Advanced aromatherapy offers a multitude of ways to support your pet's well-being, whether by creating calming environments, addressing specific health concerns, or revitalizing their energy. By carefully selecting and blending essential oils, you can target a range of issues, from anxiety to pain relief to behavioral challenges, all while enhancing the bond between you and your pet. With a mindful approach to the use of these powerful natural remedies, aromatherapy becomes a gentle yet transformative part of your pet's holistic care regimen, bringing both physical healing and emotional peace.

Chapter 5
Reiki for Animals
Channeling Energy for Healing

Reiki, a Japanese energy healing practice, has become an increasingly popular method for promoting well-being in animals. This gentle, non-invasive technique involves channeling universal life energy—known as "ki" or "chi"—to help restore balance and harmony to the body. In animals, Reiki can be used to support healing, reduce stress, and enhance emotional well-being, making it an excellent complementary therapy for both physical and behavioral issues.

At its core, Reiki is based on the belief that all living beings have an innate energy field that influences their health and vitality. When this energy is flowing freely, the body is in a state of balance, allowing it to heal naturally and function optimally. However, when the energy becomes blocked or stagnant—whether due to physical illness, emotional trauma, or environmental stress—disruptions occur, leading to discomfort or disease. Reiki works to clear these blockages and restore the natural flow of energy, allowing the body to return to its natural state of balance.

One of the greatest strengths of Reiki is its versatility. Unlike some therapies that require physical touch, Reiki can be performed either hands-on or from a distance, making it ideal for animals who are shy, anxious, or uncomfortable with handling. In fact, many animals are highly receptive to the calming energy of Reiki, often responding with visible signs of relaxation during a session—such as softening of the eyes, a relaxed posture, or even falling asleep. For this reason, Reiki is especially helpful for pets that may be recovering from surgery, dealing with chronic pain, or experiencing emotional stress.

To begin practicing Reiki with your pet, it's important to create a calm and quiet environment where both you and the animal feel relaxed and centered. This can be a designated healing space in your home or simply a quiet room where the pet feels safe. Begin by sitting near your pet and taking a few deep breaths to center yourself. You may want to place your hands on or near your pet's body, but remember that physical contact is not necessary for Reiki to be effective. The intention behind your practice—sending healing energy to your pet—is what truly matters.

During a Reiki session, it's important to remain attuned to your pet's energy and responses. Some animals may prefer a hands-off approach, while others might seek out physical touch during the session. Be flexible and allow the pet to guide the process. Reiki practitioners often describe feeling a gentle warmth or tingling sensation in their hands as the energy flows, which can indicate areas of the body where healing is most needed.

As you channel Reiki energy to your pet, focus on the intention of healing and balance. You may find it helpful to visualize the energy flowing through your hands and into the pet's body, clearing any blockages and filling them with light and warmth. This process can be particularly effective when addressing specific health concerns or areas of the body where the pet is experiencing discomfort. For example, if your dog has arthritis in its hips, you might direct the energy toward that area, visualizing the joints becoming loose and flexible, with the pain and stiffness dissolving away.

Reiki is also a powerful tool for emotional healing, particularly for pets who have experienced trauma or neglect. Many rescue animals carry deep emotional wounds that manifest as fear, anxiety, or behavioral issues. Reiki can help these animals release emotional blockages, allowing them to feel safe, loved, and supported. When working with an emotionally distressed animal, it's important to approach the session with a sense of compassion and patience, giving the pet the space they need to open up to the healing energy.

Reiki sessions can vary in length, depending on the needs of the animal and how receptive they are to the energy. Some sessions may last only 10 to 15 minutes, while others can go longer. It's important to let the pet dictate the pace—when they have received enough energy, they will often signal that the session is complete by moving away or falling into a deep, restful sleep. After the session, you may notice positive changes in your pet's mood, behavior, or physical condition, as the energy continues to work within their body over the following days.

Reiki is not meant to replace traditional veterinary care but to complement it, providing an additional layer of support that addresses the pet's energetic and emotional needs. For animals undergoing medical treatment, Reiki can help reduce stress, promote faster healing, and alleviate side effects from medications or procedures. When combined with other holistic treatments, such as aromatherapy or massage, Reiki offers a well-rounded approach to healing that considers the animal's whole being—physical, emotional, and energetic.

Building on the basics of Reiki introduced in the previous chapter, we now explore advanced techniques that can deepen your practice and enhance the healing effects for your pet. Reiki, while inherently simple, has various levels of mastery, and with practice, one can access more profound layers of healing by working with specific symbols and focusing on the animal's chakras. These methods can help unblock deep-seated energetic disruptions, amplify the flow of healing energy, and address complex emotional and physical issues that may be affecting your pet.

Reiki symbols are powerful tools used by practitioners to focus and direct healing energy. Traditionally, these symbols are introduced as the practitioner progresses through different levels of Reiki training. For animal Reiki, these symbols can help target specific energetic imbalances, allowing for a more focused and intense healing experience. There are three main symbols commonly used in Reiki practice: Cho Ku Rei (the Power Symbol), Sei He Ki (the Emotional Healing Symbol), and Hon

Sha Ze Sho Nen (the Distance Healing Symbol). Each symbol serves a unique purpose in enhancing the flow of energy and addressing particular areas of concern in the pet's body or energy field.

The Cho Ku Rei symbol is often referred to as the "power switch" of Reiki, as it helps to intensify and focus the healing energy being channeled. This symbol can be particularly useful when working with areas of the body that are experiencing physical pain or stagnation. For example, if your pet has a chronic injury or condition such as arthritis, using the Cho Ku Rei symbol during a Reiki session can help to magnify the energy directed toward the affected area, promoting deeper healing and faster relief. To use this symbol, visualize it in your mind while focusing on the part of the pet's body that requires healing, or draw the symbol with your hand in the air above the pet's body.

The Sei He Ki symbol is used for emotional and mental healing, making it an especially valuable tool for animals dealing with anxiety, trauma, or behavioral issues. This symbol helps to balance the energy of the mind and emotions, allowing pets to release fear, stress, or emotional blockages that may be contributing to their discomfort. Animals that have experienced neglect, abuse, or major life changes can benefit greatly from the use of the Sei He Ki symbol, as it works to harmonize emotional energies and create a sense of inner peace. During a Reiki session, you can use this symbol to focus on your pet's heart or solar plexus chakra, both of which are linked to emotional well-being.

The Hon Sha Ze Sho Nen symbol is used for distance healing, allowing Reiki practitioners to send healing energy across space and time. This symbol is particularly helpful if you are unable to be physically present with your pet or if you wish to send healing energy to an animal that is far away, such as a rescue animal in another location or a pet undergoing surgery while you wait at home. By visualizing this symbol, you can direct Reiki energy to the animal regardless of their physical location, allowing for the same profound healing benefits as an in-person session. Distance healing is also useful for pets who are too anxious or sensitive to receive hands-on Reiki, as it provides a gentle, non-invasive way to support their energy field from a distance.

Incorporating Reiki symbols into your practice can deepen the healing experience, allowing for more focused and targeted energy work. However, it's important to remember that the intention behind the healing session is just as powerful as the symbols themselves. Whether or not you use symbols, maintaining a clear, focused intention of love and healing is what ultimately channels the energy most effectively. Animals are highly sensitive to intention, and they respond best when the energy is pure and compassionate.

In addition to using Reiki symbols, advanced practitioners often focus on specific chakras during a session to address deeper energetic imbalances. As discussed in earlier chapters, animals have chakras just like humans, and these energy centers govern different aspects of their physical, emotional, and spiritual well-being. By working with the chakras, you can help unblock stagnant energy, promote healing, and restore balance to your pet's entire energy system.

When performing Reiki on animals, it's helpful to have a basic understanding of the chakras and their corresponding locations in the pet's body. For example, the Root Chakra, located at the base of the spine, governs physical stability, security, and grounding. If your pet is experiencing fear, anxiety, or instability, working with the Root Chakra can help restore a sense of safety and calm. Similarly, the Heart Chakra, located at the center of the chest, governs love, compassion, and emotional connection. Animals that are recovering from emotional trauma or struggling with behavioral issues related to fear or mistrust often benefit from Reiki focused on the Heart Chakra.

To perform chakra-focused Reiki, begin by placing your hands over the area where the chakra is located. For example, if you are working with the Solar Plexus Chakra, which is located just below the ribcage and governs confidence and personal power, you can place your hands on or near this area of your pet's body. As you channel Reiki energy, visualize the chakra spinning gently and smoothly, free of blockages or imbalances. You may also use Reiki symbols in conjunction with chakra work, particularly the Sei He Ki symbol for emotional healing or the Cho Ku Rei symbol to amplify the energy flow through the chakra.

Another advanced technique in animal Reiki is grounding. Grounding helps to anchor both the pet and the practitioner's energy to the earth, creating stability and balance. This technique is particularly useful for pets that are anxious, overly energetic, or have trouble settling down. To ground your pet during a Reiki session, focus on their Root Chakra and visualize a cord of energy extending from this chakra down into the earth. Imagine this energy cord connecting your pet to the earth's core, helping to draw away any excess or scattered energy and replacing it with calm, stabilizing energy. You can also perform grounding by placing your hands gently on your pet's paws or near the base of their spine, encouraging the flow of energy downward.

Grounding is not only beneficial for pets but also for practitioners. Because Reiki practitioners serve as conduits for healing energy, it's important to remain grounded during the session to prevent becoming overwhelmed or drained by the flow of energy. Before and after a Reiki session, take a moment to ground yourself by placing your feet firmly on the floor, taking a few deep breaths, and visualizing your own energy connecting with the earth. This practice ensures that the energy exchange remains balanced and that both you and your pet feel calm and centered throughout the process.

The benefits of Reiki extend far beyond physical healing. Many pet owners report that regular Reiki sessions help to deepen the emotional bond between them and their animals. Because Reiki operates on such a gentle, energetic level, it allows for a profound exchange of love and trust between pet and owner. As you continue to practice Reiki with your pet, you may notice that they become more receptive to your energy and more attuned to your emotional state. This mutual connection creates a sense of harmony and balance that can enhance your relationship in powerful ways.

In addition to using Reiki for specific health concerns or emotional issues, it can also be used as part of a preventive wellness routine. Regular Reiki sessions help to maintain the free flow of energy throughout your pet's body, preventing blockages from forming and keeping their energy field vibrant and balanced. For older pets or those with chronic conditions, Reiki can help alleviate discomfort and improve quality of life, while for younger or more active animals, it can support overall well-being and emotional stability.

Incorporating advanced Reiki techniques into your pet's holistic care routine allows for a more comprehensive and personalized approach to healing. Whether you're using symbols to intensify the energy flow, focusing on chakra balancing, or practicing grounding techniques, Reiki offers a flexible and powerful tool for supporting your pet's health and happiness. Over time, as you continue to work with these techniques, you'll likely find that your pet becomes more responsive to the healing energy, and the positive effects of Reiki will become more pronounced in their overall well-being.

Chapter 6
Chromotherapy
The Power of Colors in Animal Health

Chromotherapy, also known as color therapy, is a form of healing that uses the vibrational energy of colors to influence physical, emotional, and energetic health. Each color carries a unique wavelength and frequency, which can have specific effects on the body and mind. In the realm of animal health, chromotherapy offers a non-invasive and gentle way to balance energy, reduce stress, and promote healing by introducing the appropriate colors into a pet's environment or treatment plan.

Animals, like humans, are sensitive to the energies around them, and color plays a significant role in how they perceive and respond to their surroundings. By understanding the effects that different colors have on the body's energy field, you can use chromotherapy to create a healing and supportive environment for your pet. For example, blue is often associated with calmness and relaxation, making it an ideal choice for anxious or stressed pets. Conversely, red is linked to energy and vitality, which can be useful for animals that need a boost in energy or are recovering from illness.

The principle behind chromotherapy is that each color resonates with a specific energy center (chakra) in the body, and by exposing the body to the right color, you can restore balance to these energy centers. For instance, red is connected to the Root Chakra, which governs physical stability and grounding, while green corresponds to the Heart Chakra, which is associated with love and emotional healing. By using colors that resonate with a particular chakra, you can help clear blockages and enhance the flow of energy through that energy center.

One of the simplest ways to incorporate chromotherapy into your pet's life is through environmental color therapy. This can be achieved by introducing objects, fabrics, or lighting in specific colors into your pet's living space. For example, if your pet suffers from anxiety, you might add blue or green blankets, bedding, or toys to their space, creating a calm and soothing environment that promotes relaxation. Alternatively, for a pet recovering from surgery or illness, you might introduce red or orange elements to their environment to stimulate energy and healing.

In addition to creating a color-balanced environment, you can also use colored lights as part of a chromotherapy session. Specially designed chromotherapy lamps or LED lights that emit specific colors can be used to target your pet's energy centers during a healing session. For example, bathing an animal in soft blue light can help reduce stress and anxiety, while green light can be used to promote emotional healing, particularly for animals recovering from trauma or neglect.

When working with colored lights, it's important to create a calm and controlled environment where the animal feels safe. Begin by dimming any other lights in the room and introducing the colored light gradually, allowing your pet to adjust to the new sensation. You can aim the light at specific parts of the body corresponding to the chakras you are working on, or simply allow the light to fill the space around the pet. Be mindful of your pet's reactions—if they seem uneasy or avoid the light, try reducing the intensity or choosing a different color.

Chromotherapy can also be integrated into other holistic treatments, such as Reiki or massage. For example, during a Reiki session, you might enhance the energy work by placing a colored blanket that corresponds to the chakra you're focusing on. If you're working on the Root Chakra, a red blanket can help amplify the grounding energy of that chakra, while a green blanket can support heart-centered healing during a Heart Chakra session. This combination of energy work and color therapy can create a more immersive and effective healing experience.

Another way to use chromotherapy is through colored crystals, which are often used in crystal healing to amplify the effects of specific colors. For example, placing a red jasper crystal near your pet can help stimulate the Root Chakra, while an amethyst crystal can aid in calming the mind and supporting the Third Eye Chakra. By strategically placing these crystals in your pet's environment or during healing sessions, you can support the flow of energy in a targeted and powerful way.

Deepening your understanding and application of chromotherapy can unlock even greater healing potential for your pet. As discussed earlier, colors have unique vibrational frequencies that correspond to different physical, emotional, and energetic states. By strategically applying these colors using various tools—such as colored lamps, crystals, and objects—you can target specific ailments or imbalances in your pet's energy field and promote overall well-being. This chapter will explore how to implement chromotherapy in a more structured and intentional way, focusing on practical methods to create a harmonious environment for your pet.

One of the most effective ways to incorporate chromotherapy into your pet's daily life is by using colored lamps or light bulbs. Specially designed chromotherapy lamps or even colored LED lights can be used to bathe your pet in healing light, either during focused sessions or as part of their regular environment. These lights can help create a soothing atmosphere that supports healing and emotional balance, especially when combined with other holistic practices like Reiki, massage, or aromatherapy.

To begin using colored lamps, it's important to choose the right color for your pet's specific needs. For example, blue light is incredibly soothing and can be beneficial for pets experiencing anxiety, restlessness, or hyperactivity. Blue light reduces stress and creates a calming effect, making it ideal for pets recovering from trauma or adjusting to new environments. If you have a high-strung or anxious dog, consider using blue light therapy in their sleeping area to help them relax and get better rest.

On the other hand, if your pet is lethargic, fatigued, or recovering from illness, red light can be used to stimulate energy and promote vitality. Red light is associated with the Root Chakra, which governs physical strength, stability, and grounding. Bathing a pet in soft red light for short periods of time can help boost circulation and increase physical energy. This is particularly useful for older pets or those with chronic conditions like arthritis, as it helps improve mobility and reduces pain.

Green light is another versatile option in chromotherapy, as it resonates with the Heart Chakra and is associated with balance, healing, and emotional calm. Green is known to promote healing on a physical and emotional level, making it a great choice for pets recovering from injury or surgery. It can also be used to help pets that are experiencing grief or separation anxiety. Placing a green light in a room where your pet spends a lot of time can create an overall sense of peace and emotional stability.

When using colored lamps, it's important to monitor your pet's response. Animals are highly sensitive to light and energy, and while many pets enjoy the soothing effects of colored lights, others may feel overstimulated if the lights are too bright or used for too long. Start with short sessions, around 10-15 minutes, and observe your pet's behavior. If they seem relaxed or drawn to the light, you can gradually increase the duration. If they seem uncomfortable, restless, or avoid the area, try a different color or reduce the intensity of the light.

Another powerful tool in chromotherapy is the use of crystals, which carry specific energetic frequencies that correspond to the chakras and can amplify the healing effects of color. Crystals like amethyst, rose quartz, and citrine can be placed in your pet's environment or used directly during healing sessions to balance their energy. For example, amethyst, a violet-colored crystal, is associated with the Third Eye Chakra and is known for its calming and protective properties. Placing an amethyst crystal near your pet's bed or resting area can help promote relaxation and enhance mental clarity.

Rose quartz, a pink stone associated with the Heart Chakra, is another excellent crystal for pets, especially those recovering from emotional trauma or neglect. It promotes love, compassion, and emotional healing, making it ideal for pets that are fearful, anxious, or withdrawn. You can place rose quartz stones in areas where your pet spends the most time, such as their bed or favorite resting spot, to help infuse the space with calming, heart-centered energy.

Citrine, a yellow-golden crystal, is associated with the Solar Plexus Chakra, which governs confidence, personal power, and vitality. For pets that are recovering from illness or need an energy boost, placing citrine stones near their food or water bowls, or using them during massage or Reiki sessions, can help energize and revitalize them. Citrine is also known for its protective properties and can help shield sensitive animals from negative energies in their environment.

In addition to using crystals, you can also incorporate colored objects into your pet's environment to reinforce the desired energetic effects. For example, introducing colored bedding, toys, or collars that correspond to the healing properties you want to focus on can subtly influence your pet's energy over time. A blue collar can help calm an anxious dog, while red or orange bedding can stimulate energy and vitality in an older or fatigued pet. Surrounding your pet with colors that resonate with their energy needs creates a harmonious environment that supports long-term balance and well-being.

One of the simplest ways to use color in your pet's environment is by selecting items that naturally incorporate healing colors, such as food and water bowls, blankets, or even toys. These everyday objects can become tools of healing when chosen with intention. For example, a green blanket can promote healing and emotional balance, while a blue or violet toy can help calm an overstimulated or hyperactive pet. Over time, the regular exposure to these colors will create a subtle yet powerful shift in your pet's energy.

It's important to remember that chromotherapy, like any holistic treatment, works best when tailored to the individual needs of the pet. No two animals are exactly the same, and what works well for one may not have the same effect on another. Pay attention to your pet's behavior and reactions to different colors, adjusting your approach as necessary to find the combination that best supports their health and well-being.

Chromotherapy can also be integrated into other holistic practices. For example, you can combine colored light therapy with aromatherapy, using essential oils that correspond to the color's energy. Diffusing lavender essential oil while using blue light, for instance, can enhance the calming effects of both treatments. Similarly, combining green light therapy with Reiki focused on the Heart Chakra can amplify emotional healing and release blockages. This integrative approach allows for a more comprehensive and personalized healing experience.

In conclusion, chromotherapy offers a versatile and gentle way to promote health and balance in your pet's life. By using colored lights, crystals, and objects strategically, you can target specific energy centers, relieve stress, and support physical and emotional healing. Whether you're addressing anxiety, physical pain, or emotional trauma, the power of color can be a valuable tool in your pet's holistic care routine. Over time, these practices can create a more peaceful, balanced, and harmonious environment for your pet, contributing to their overall well-being.

Chapter 7
Balancing Chakras and Energies

Crystal therapy, also known as crystal healing, is an ancient practice that harnesses the natural vibrations of gemstones to influence and balance energy within the body. Animals, like humans, have their own energetic systems, including chakras that can become blocked or unbalanced due to stress, illness, or environmental factors. By using crystals, pet owners can support their pets' physical and emotional well-being, creating harmony within their energy fields. In this chapter, we will explore the basics of crystal therapy for pets, focusing on specific stones that are beneficial for balancing energy, calming emotional distress, and promoting healing.

Crystals are believed to hold specific vibrational frequencies that resonate with the body's energy centers. Each crystal has unique properties that can influence certain aspects of health, whether it be calming anxiety, boosting energy, or aiding in recovery from illness. By placing crystals near a pet's body or in their environment, we can help align their chakras and support their natural healing processes.

The first step in using crystal therapy with animals is selecting the appropriate stones based on the pet's specific needs. Different crystals are associated with different chakras, each governing various aspects of physical and emotional well-being. For example, rose quartz, a gentle pink stone, is often used to promote emotional healing and open the Heart Chakra. This makes it an excellent choice for pets experiencing emotional distress, such as those recovering from trauma or dealing with separation anxiety. By placing rose quartz near your pet's bed or on their collar (using a small, safe pendant), you can help create a soothing, loving energy that supports emotional balance.

Amethyst, a violet-colored stone, is another powerful crystal that resonates with the Crown and Third Eye Chakras. Known for its calming and protective properties, amethyst is commonly used to reduce stress and anxiety in pets. It can also help enhance mental clarity and support spiritual connection, making it ideal for animals that are highly sensitive or prone to stress. If your pet struggles with hyperactivity or nervousness, placing amethyst in their environment or using it during a healing session can help calm their energy and bring them into a more relaxed state.

Citrine, a bright yellow-golden crystal, is associated with the Solar Plexus Chakra, which governs confidence, personal power, and vitality. For pets that seem sluggish, lethargic, or lacking in energy, citrine can help stimulate their natural energy and revitalize their spirit. This crystal is also known for its ability to promote happiness and positivity, making it a great tool for pets that are recovering from illness or dealing with long-term emotional issues. Citrine can be placed near your pet's feeding area or in their favorite play space to encourage physical and emotional revitalization.

Clear quartz is often called the "master healer" of crystals because of its versatile and amplifying properties. Clear quartz resonates with all the chakras, making it useful for general healing and energy balancing. It helps to amplify the energy of other crystals, meaning it can be paired with any other stone to enhance its effects. For pets dealing with complex health issues or multiple imbalances, clear quartz can serve as a foundational crystal, helping to clear energetic blockages and promote overall harmony. Simply placing clear quartz near your pet's bed or using it during a massage or Reiki session can help support their holistic well-being.

In addition to these crystals, there are many other stones that can be used to target specific conditions or energetic imbalances in animals. For example, black tourmaline is a powerful grounding stone that helps protect against negative energy and electromagnetic pollution. This makes it ideal for pets that live in busy urban environments or spend a lot of time indoors around electronic devices. Placing black tourmaline in your pet's living space can help shield them from excess energy and keep them grounded.

Another commonly used crystal is green aventurine, which is associated with the Heart Chakra and is known for its ability to promote physical healing and emotional recovery. For pets recovering from surgery or dealing with chronic health conditions, green aventurine can help speed up the healing process and provide comfort during recovery. It can be placed near the pet during rest or healing sessions to encourage faster physical and emotional recovery.

Once you've selected the right crystals for your pet, it's important to know how to use them effectively. One of the most common ways to use crystals in animal healing is by placing them in the pet's environment, such as their sleeping area, feeding space, or play zone. By surrounding the pet with crystals that resonate with their specific energy needs, you create a healing environment that continuously supports their well-being.

Crystals can also be used in direct healing sessions, such as during Reiki, massage, or meditation. During these sessions, the practitioner can place the crystal directly on or near the pet's body, focusing on the chakra that needs balancing. For example, placing a rose quartz stone on the pet's chest during a Reiki session can help open and balance the Heart Chakra, promoting emotional healing and fostering a stronger bond between the pet and owner.

It's important to approach crystal therapy with care and attention to the pet's comfort and sensitivity. Animals are naturally attuned to energy, and while some pets may respond positively to the presence of crystals, others may be more sensitive or resistant. Start by introducing the crystals gradually and observing your pet's reactions. If your pet seems relaxed or drawn to the crystal, you can continue using it in their environment. However, if your pet shows signs of discomfort or avoidance, it may be best to remove the crystal and try a different stone or method.

In addition to using crystals for healing sessions, you can create crystal grids around your pet's space to amplify the effects of the stones. A crystal grid is a specific arrangement of crystals designed to focus and enhance the flow of energy. By placing the crystals in a geometric pattern around your pet's bed or play area, you can create an energy field that continuously promotes healing and balance. This is particularly useful for pets with chronic conditions or ongoing emotional issues, as the grid works passively over time to support their energy.

Another important aspect of crystal therapy is keeping the stones cleansed and charged. Crystals absorb and store energy, and over time, they can become energetically depleted or hold onto negative energy. To keep your crystals effective, it's important to cleanse them regularly. This can be done by placing the crystals in sunlight or moonlight for a few hours, smudging them with sage or palo santo, or placing them in a bowl of sea salt. Once cleansed, the crystals can be charged with your intention by holding them in your hands and visualizing the energy you wish them to carry.

Crystal therapy offers a gentle and non-invasive way to support your pet's physical, emotional, and energetic health. By selecting the appropriate crystals and using them in a mindful, intentional manner, you can help balance your pet's chakras, alleviate stress, and promote healing. Whether you use crystals in your pet's environment, during healing sessions, or as part of a larger holistic regimen, this practice can enhance their overall well-being and create a more harmonious life for your beloved companion.

Having introduced the basic principles of crystal therapy and the types of stones that can benefit pets, we now deepen the exploration of this holistic practice by focusing on specific methods for applying crystals to heal particular ailments and balance unsteady chakras. This chapter will guide you through the practical use of crystals to directly influence your pet's energy field, including techniques for positioning crystals on or around the pet's body, creating crystal grids, and combining crystal therapy with other holistic treatments for a comprehensive healing experience.

One of the most effective ways to harness the power of crystals for your pet's healing is by placing them directly on or near the animal's body, targeting specific chakras that need balancing. As discussed previously, each chakra corresponds to different aspects of an animal's physical and emotional health, and certain crystals resonate with these energy centers. For example, placing a piece of rose quartz on the chest area aligns with the Heart Chakra, promoting emotional healing and love, while a piece of citrine near the belly resonates with the Solar Plexus Chakra, boosting energy and confidence.

When placing crystals on your pet, it's crucial to ensure that the experience is gentle and non-invasive. Begin by placing the pet in a calm, relaxed state, perhaps after a walk or playtime, or during their usual nap time. Once they are comfortable, start by placing the crystals gently on or near the chakras you want to focus on. For example, if your pet is dealing with digestive issues or lack of energy, place citrine or amber near their stomach, corresponding to the Solar Plexus Chakra. If your pet is anxious or emotionally unsettled, rose quartz or green aventurine placed on their chest can help balance the Heart Chakra, encouraging a sense of peace and comfort.

It's important to keep the session short, especially when first introducing crystals. Begin with five to ten minutes, observing your pet's behavior and reactions. Some animals may enjoy the sensation and even move closer to the crystals, while others may be indifferent or mildly resistant. If your pet seems uncomfortable, remove the crystal and allow them to adjust at their own pace. Over time, as your pet becomes more familiar with crystal healing, you can extend the sessions gradually.

Beyond placing crystals directly on your pet's body, you can also enhance the healing process by creating crystal grids around their environment. Crystal grids are arrangements of stones in specific geometric patterns that amplify the healing energy of the crystals. This technique is particularly useful for pets that may not tolerate direct contact with stones but still benefit from the vibrational energy in their space. A crystal grid can be created around your pet's bed, favorite resting spot, or any area where they spend a lot of time.

To create a crystal grid, choose the stones based on the areas of healing you wish to focus on. For instance, if your pet is recovering from surgery or illness, you might use green aventurine, clear quartz, and amethyst—each known for their healing and regenerative properties. Place the crystals in a symmetrical pattern around your pet's bed or resting area, with clear quartz at the center to amplify the effects of the surrounding stones. As your pet rests within the grid, the combined energy of the stones will promote healing and balance, encouraging recovery and well-being.

For animals that experience chronic conditions like arthritis, you can set up a permanent or semi-permanent grid around their bed, using stones that aid in pain relief and energy flow. Stones like amber, hematite, and smoky quartz can help reduce inflammation and pain, while supporting the pet's overall vitality. You can recharge the grid by regularly cleansing the crystals and resetting your healing intention.

In addition to static crystal grids, you can also create portable grids by arranging smaller stones in a cloth pouch or small container that you can place near your pet's bed or carry with them when traveling or visiting the vet. These portable grids can be particularly helpful for pets that experience anxiety or discomfort in new environments, as the energy of the stones will provide a constant source of comfort and balance no matter where they are.

Another powerful method of incorporating crystals into your pet's healing routine is through water charging. This involves placing crystals around or inside your pet's water dish (be cautious not to use any toxic stones) to infuse the water with healing energy. Stones such as rose quartz, amethyst, or clear quartz are safe for this purpose and can charge the water with calming, healing vibrations. This can be especially useful for pets dealing with emotional stress, as drinking water that has been charged with crystals can help calm their nervous system and promote emotional balance from within.

To charge water with crystal energy, simply place a clean, non-toxic crystal in or near your pet's water bowl for a few hours. The stone will imbue the water with its healing properties, which the pet then absorbs as they drink. Be sure to research which crystals are safe for direct water exposure—some stones, like malachite, are toxic when submerged in water and should be avoided. If in doubt, place the crystals near the bowl rather than in it.

Crystal therapy can also be integrated with other holistic treatments such as Reiki, aromatherapy, and massage to enhance the overall healing effect. During a Reiki session, placing crystals on or near the pet's chakras can help intensify the flow of energy and clear any blockages more efficiently. For example, using amethyst during a Reiki session focused on the Crown Chakra can deepen the pet's connection to higher energy and promote mental clarity and peace. Similarly, combining crystal therapy with aromatherapy—by diffusing essential oils while using crystals—can create a soothing, multi-sensory experience that amplifies relaxation and healing.

Massage is another modality that pairs well with crystal healing. During a massage session, you can place specific stones along the pet's spine or on key chakra points, allowing the energy from the crystals to penetrate deeper into the body as you work to relax the muscles and release tension. This combination not only addresses physical discomfort but also promotes energetic balance, making the massage session more holistic and effective.

As with any healing practice, it's essential to regularly cleanse and recharge your crystals to ensure that they continue to work at their highest potential. Crystals absorb energy from their surroundings, and over time, they may become energetically "clogged" or depleted. Cleansing can be done by placing the crystals in sunlight or moonlight for a few hours, smudging them with sage or palo santo, or immersing them in a bowl of sea salt. After cleansing, recharging the stones with your intention is important—hold the crystal in your hand and focus on the specific healing you want it to provide.

Finally, always approach crystal therapy with an open heart and patience, understanding that animals, like humans, have their own unique energy systems and responses. Some pets may respond quickly to crystal healing, while others may take more time to adjust. The key is to observe and remain attuned to your pet's needs, gradually incorporating crystals into their environment and care routine in a way that feels natural and supportive.

By integrating crystals into your pet's holistic care, you provide a powerful, non-invasive method to support physical healing, emotional balance, and energetic well-being. Whether used alone or in combination with other therapies, crystals offer a gentle yet profound way to enhance your pet's quality of life, helping them maintain harmony in body, mind, and spirit. Through consistent practice and mindful application, crystal therapy can become a valuable tool in your holistic healing toolkit, promoting a deeper connection between you and your beloved companion.

Chapter 8
Natural Diet and the Connection to Energetic Well-Being

The connection between diet and overall well-being is well-established, and this concept extends to pets as much as it does to humans. A holistic approach to pet care emphasizes the importance of nutrition not only for physical health but also for maintaining energetic balance. Just as food can provide vital nutrients for the body, it also plays a significant role in supporting the energetic systems of pets, including their chakras and emotional health. This chapter will explore the concept of natural, holistic nutrition for animals and how certain foods can promote vitality, emotional stability, and longevity.

In holistic pet care, food is viewed as both sustenance and medicine. What your pet eats directly affects their energy levels, mood, and overall health. Highly processed foods, which are common in many commercial pet diets, can disrupt the body's natural balance, leading to issues such as lethargy, anxiety, inflammation, and even behavioral problems. In contrast, a natural, whole-food diet that includes fresh, minimally processed ingredients can help align your pet's energy systems and promote a state of balance and well-being.

The first step in supporting your pet's energetic health through diet is to focus on providing high-quality, natural foods that are rich in nutrients. This includes whole proteins, healthy fats, and a variety of fruits and vegetables that provide essential vitamins, minerals, and antioxidants. Fresh, organic meats such as chicken, turkey, or fish are excellent sources of high-quality protein, which is essential for maintaining muscle mass, supporting the immune system, and providing the energy your pet needs to thrive. Additionally, including healthy fats like omega-3 and omega-6 fatty acids from sources such as fish oil, flaxseed, and chia seeds can promote healthy skin and fur, reduce inflammation, and support brain function.

Fruits and vegetables play a vital role in a pet's diet by providing the micronutrients necessary for optimal health. Dark leafy greens like spinach and kale are packed with vitamins A, C, and K, as well as minerals like iron and calcium, which are essential for bone health and immune function. Blueberries, rich in antioxidants, help combat oxidative stress and can support cognitive function in aging pets. Pumpkin, a favorite for many dogs, is an excellent source of fiber, aiding in digestion and promoting a healthy gut—an important component of both physical and emotional well-being.

The digestive system is intimately linked with the energetic systems of the body. In holistic medicine, the digestive tract is often referred to as the "second brain" due to its impact on emotional health and energy balance. A healthy gut not only ensures that your pet can absorb the nutrients they need but also supports emotional regulation and mental clarity. Foods that are high in fiber, prebiotics, and probiotics—such as pumpkin, sweet potatoes, and fermented vegetables like sauerkraut—can help maintain a healthy gut flora, which in turn supports balanced energy flow throughout the body.

In addition to whole foods, certain herbs and natural supplements can be incorporated into your pet's diet to promote energetic well-being. For example, turmeric, a powerful anti-inflammatory herb, is known to help reduce pain and inflammation, particularly in pets with arthritis or other joint issues. Its ability to support the Solar Plexus Chakra, which governs energy and vitality, makes it an excellent addition to the diet of pets who are older or experiencing fatigue. You can easily add turmeric powder to your pet's food in small amounts, mixed with a little healthy fat like coconut oil for better absorption.

Another beneficial herb is spirulina, a blue-green algae that is rich in vitamins, minerals, and amino acids. Spirulina helps detoxify the body, supports immune function, and promotes overall vitality. Energetically, it aligns with the Throat Chakra, helping to clear blockages and improve communication and expression. Adding a small amount of spirulina powder to your pet's food can support their overall energy levels and promote a sense of balance and well-being.

When considering a holistic diet for your pet, it's also important to avoid foods that can cause energetic imbalances or disrupt their health. Highly processed foods, artificial preservatives, and fillers such as corn, wheat, and soy are common in many commercial pet foods and can contribute to inflammation, digestive problems, and energy blockages. These ingredients can create "stagnant" energy, leading to lethargy or irritability, as well as more serious health issues over time. By avoiding these ingredients and focusing on whole, natural foods, you can help maintain a healthy energy flow throughout your pet's body.

A balanced diet is key to ensuring that all of your pet's chakras receive the support they need to function optimally. Just as different foods can influence physical health, they can also have specific energetic effects. For example, red-colored foods such as beets, strawberries, and lean red meats are associated with the Root Chakra, helping to ground your pet and provide a sense of security and stability. These foods are particularly beneficial for pets that are anxious, fearful, or easily stressed, as they help restore balance to the Root Chakra and promote a sense of calm.

Orange-colored foods, such as carrots, pumpkins, and sweet potatoes, resonate with the Sacral Chakra, which governs emotions, creativity, and reproductive health. These foods can help balance emotional energy, making them ideal for pets dealing with mood swings or behavioral issues. For example, if your pet is experiencing anxiety or fear-based aggression, incorporating orange-colored vegetables into their diet can help soothe emotional turbulence and promote a more balanced state of mind.

Yellow-colored foods, such as squash, bananas, and turmeric, support the Solar Plexus Chakra, which is responsible for confidence, personal power, and energy. Pets that are lethargic, lack confidence, or are recovering from illness can benefit from these foods, as they help boost vitality and encourage a more active, engaged attitude. Incorporating yellow-colored foods into your pet's diet can also enhance digestion, which is closely linked to the health of the Solar Plexus Chakra.

Green foods, such as spinach, kale, and peas, resonate with the Heart Chakra, promoting emotional healing and balance. For pets that are grieving, anxious, or have experienced trauma, green foods can help open and balance the Heart Chakra, encouraging emotional healing and a stronger connection to their environment and family. Green foods also support the immune system, making them ideal for pets that need extra support in overcoming illness or recovering from surgery.

Blue and purple foods, such as blueberries, blackberries, and purple cabbage, are associated with the Throat and Third Eye Chakras, which govern communication, intuition, and mental clarity. These foods can help pets that are shy or have difficulty expressing their needs, encouraging clearer communication and emotional expression. They are also excellent for older pets, as the antioxidants found in blue and purple foods can help protect against cognitive decline and support overall brain health.

Incorporating these colorful, whole foods into your pet's diet not only provides essential nutrients but also aligns their energy centers, promoting a balanced and harmonious state of well-being. As you develop a holistic nutrition plan for your pet, consider their individual needs, temperament, and any health issues they may be experiencing. By focusing on fresh, natural ingredients and eliminating processed, artificial foods, you can support both their physical and energetic health, ensuring a vibrant and fulfilling life.

A holistic diet that takes into account both physical and energetic needs is one of the most powerful ways to promote long-term well-being in pets. By choosing foods that nourish their bodies and align with their chakras, you create a foundation of health that supports them in every aspect of their lives. In the next chapter, we will explore how to customize a holistic diet for specific types of pets, taking into consideration their unique energetic and health requirements.

Expanding on the foundation of natural nutrition, this chapter explores how to tailor a holistic diet to meet the unique needs of different types of pets. Just as humans have individualized dietary needs based on their constitution, lifestyle, and health conditions, animals too require customized nutrition to support their energetic and physical well-being. By considering the specific characteristics of your pet—whether they are a dog, cat, rabbit, or other species—you can create a personalized diet that nourishes their body, balances their energy, and promotes long-term health.

One of the key factors in designing a holistic diet for your pet is understanding their natural dietary preferences and biological needs. Dogs, for instance, are omnivores, meaning they thrive on a diet that includes both plant-based and animal-based foods. Cats, on the other hand, are obligate carnivores, requiring a meat-based diet rich in specific nutrients such as taurine, which they cannot synthesize on their own. Rabbits, guinea pigs, and other small mammals are herbivores, depending primarily on fibrous plant material to maintain their digestive and energetic balance.

For dogs, a balanced, species-appropriate diet should include high-quality animal protein, healthy fats, and a variety of vegetables and fruits. Proteins such as chicken, turkey, beef, and fish provide the building blocks for muscle maintenance, immune support, and energy production. Adding organ meats like liver and kidney can also enhance your dog's diet, as these organs are rich in essential vitamins and minerals. Energetically, meat corresponds to the Root and Solar Plexus Chakras, promoting strength, vitality, and groundedness. Including lean, organic meats ensures your dog's Root Chakra remains balanced, fostering stability and a sense of security.

Dogs also benefit from vegetables such as carrots, broccoli, and sweet potatoes, which provide fiber, vitamins, and antioxidants to support digestion, energy, and immune function. These plant-based foods contribute to balancing the higher chakras, such as the Solar Plexus and Heart Chakras, by supporting energy flow and emotional stability. For example, orange-colored vegetables like sweet potatoes and carrots are rich in beta-carotene and resonate with the Sacral Chakra, supporting emotional balance and creativity, especially for anxious or easily overstimulated dogs.

For cats, their diet must focus primarily on meat to meet their nutritional needs as obligate carnivores. High-quality animal protein is critical for maintaining their energy levels, muscle mass, and overall vitality. Foods like chicken, turkey, beef, and fish provide essential amino acids and nutrients like taurine, which are crucial for heart health, vision, and neurological function. Fish, in particular, is a great source of omega-3 fatty acids, which support the health of the nervous system, reduce inflammation, and promote skin and coat health.

Cats benefit from a diet that is low in carbohydrates and high in protein, as this closely mimics their natural diet in the wild. Too many carbohydrates can lead to weight gain, digestive issues, and energy imbalances. A diet rich in raw or lightly cooked meats, supplemented with natural oils like fish oil, ensures that your cat receives the nutrition they need to stay energetic, healthy, and balanced. The high-protein content of meat naturally energizes the Solar Plexus and Root Chakras, supporting confidence, vitality, and physical grounding.

For rabbits, guinea pigs, and other small herbivores, the focus should be on providing a variety of fibrous plants to support their delicate digestive systems. These animals require a diet rich in hay, leafy greens, and fresh vegetables to maintain the proper balance of nutrients and energy. Hay, particularly timothy or meadow hay, is the staple of their diet, providing the fiber necessary for digestive health. Vegetables like lettuce, kale, and parsley provide additional nutrients and energy to support their body and mind. For herbivorous animals, green foods are especially important for balancing the Heart Chakra, which governs emotional stability and connection.

Herbivores also benefit from root vegetables like carrots and turnips, which resonate with the Root Chakra and provide grounding energy. These foods help maintain a healthy balance between physical health and emotional well-being, particularly for animals that are prone to anxiety or stress in captivity. A diet rich in natural, fibrous plants helps these animals maintain the vitality of their digestive system, which in turn supports balanced energy flow throughout their entire body.

In addition to understanding species-specific dietary needs, it's important to consider your pet's individual health and energetic profile when designing their diet. Some animals may have sensitivities or allergies to certain foods, requiring adjustments to avoid ingredients that could cause digestive upset or inflammation. For example, some dogs are sensitive to grains or dairy, which can lead to skin issues, digestive problems, or energy imbalances. If you suspect your pet has food sensitivities, consider working with a holistic veterinarian to identify any allergens and adjust their diet accordingly.

Pets with chronic conditions, such as arthritis, kidney disease, or digestive disorders, can also benefit from specific dietary adjustments to support their healing and maintain energetic balance. For example, pets with joint pain or arthritis may benefit from anti-inflammatory foods like turmeric, ginger, and omega-3-rich fish oils. These ingredients help reduce inflammation and pain while also supporting the Solar Plexus and Sacral Chakras, promoting flexibility, movement, and vitality.

For pets with kidney disease, reducing protein and phosphorus levels in their diet may be necessary to ease the strain on the kidneys while still providing the nutrients they need. Incorporating easily digestible proteins like chicken or turkey, along with vegetables such as carrots and sweet potatoes, can help maintain energy without overloading the kidneys. Energetically, foods that support the lower chakras, such as the Root and Sacral

Chakras, can help pets with kidney disease maintain physical strength and emotional stability during their treatment.

Pets experiencing anxiety, stress, or behavioral issues can benefit from calming foods that resonate with the Heart and Solar Plexus Chakras. Adding foods like chamomile, which can be brewed into a tea and added to your pet's water or food, can help soothe their nervous system and promote emotional balance. Chamomile's calming properties are well-known, and its energetic resonance with the Heart Chakra makes it ideal for pets dealing with separation anxiety, nervousness, or emotional distress.

Another key consideration in creating a holistic diet is the inclusion of supplements that support your pet's energetic and physical needs. Omega-3 fatty acids from fish oil or flaxseed oil are excellent for promoting brain health, reducing inflammation, and supporting skin and coat health. For pets that need an immune boost, adding supplements like spirulina, chlorella, or medicinal mushrooms (such as reishi or shiitake) can enhance their immune response and support overall vitality. These supplements resonate with the Crown and Throat Chakras, helping to maintain a clear, balanced flow of energy throughout the body.

For animals recovering from surgery or illness, consider incorporating bone broth into their diet. Bone broth is rich in collagen, amino acids, and minerals that support joint health, digestion, and immune function. It's also easy to digest and can be a comforting, nourishing food for pets with decreased appetites. Energetically, bone broth resonates with the Root Chakra, helping pets regain their physical strength and groundedness during recovery.

Hydration is another critical component of your pet's holistic diet. Ensuring that your pet drinks enough water helps maintain energetic balance, as dehydration can lead to sluggish energy flow and physical fatigue. In addition to clean, fresh water, you can offer your pet hydrating foods like cucumber, watermelon, and broth-based soups to increase their water intake.

These hydrating foods resonate with the Sacral Chakra, which governs fluidity and emotional balance.

Finally, in developing a holistic diet for your pet, always remember to listen to your pet's body and energy. Animals are intuitive beings, and they often know what foods make them feel good. Pay attention to their energy levels, digestion, and behavior, and adjust their diet as needed to support their changing needs over time. A holistic diet is not static but evolves with your pet's life stages, health, and environment, ensuring that they continue to thrive both physically and energetically.

In conclusion, tailoring a holistic, natural diet to your pet's specific needs supports their energetic and physical well-being, helping them maintain balance in body, mind, and spirit. By choosing fresh, whole foods and avoiding processed ingredients, you provide the foundation for vibrant health and longevity. In the next chapter, we will explore the role of music therapy in enhancing your pet's emotional and energetic health, focusing on how sound and healing frequencies can influence their mood, behavior, and overall well-being.

Chapter 9
Music Therapy
Healing Sounds

Music therapy is an increasingly recognized tool in holistic pet care, offering a non-invasive, gentle way to influence the emotional and energetic state of animals. Sound, in its various forms, carries vibrational frequencies that can directly impact the nervous system, calming or energizing the body depending on the chosen tone, rhythm, and tempo. Just as humans respond to certain types of music with relaxation, focus, or revitalization, animals, too, are highly sensitive to sound, making music therapy an effective method for supporting their emotional and energetic well-being.

Sound has a direct impact on an animal's energy field, and by carefully selecting the right types of music or frequencies, you can address issues like anxiety, stress, hyperactivity, and even aggression. This chapter will explore how sound influences animals' emotions and energy, introducing the basics of music therapy and guiding you in choosing the appropriate types of music for different purposes. Whether your goal is to calm a nervous dog, soothe an anxious cat, or boost your pet's energy, music therapy provides a natural, holistic option.

The science behind music therapy lies in the vibrational frequencies of sound. All living beings, including animals, are surrounded by and connected to their energetic fields, or biofields. These fields resonate with external vibrations, including sound waves. When an animal is stressed or anxious, its energy field can become erratic or unbalanced. Playing certain types of music—particularly those that produce slow, calming rhythms—can help stabilize and harmonize these energy fields, promoting relaxation and emotional balance.

One of the most effective uses of music therapy for pets is in reducing anxiety and stress. Pets often experience heightened anxiety during specific situations, such as thunderstorms, fireworks, visits to the vet, or being left alone. For animals prone to these stressors, playing calming music with slow tempos, soft melodies, and consistent rhythms can help lower their stress levels by synchronizing their heart rate and breathing to the rhythm of the music.

Classical music is one of the most commonly recommended genres for calming pets, particularly works by composers like Beethoven or Mozart. These pieces often feature gentle harmonies and soothing, repetitive patterns, which can help create a sense of security and peace. Studies have shown that dogs, for example, respond well to classical music, with reduced barking, heart rate, and overall stress levels. Playing classical music in the background while your pet rests or during stressful events can help maintain a calm environment, allowing your pet's nervous system to settle.

Another genre that works particularly well for pets is soft ambient music. Ambient music, often characterized by slow, evolving soundscapes with little to no abrupt changes, provides a continuous flow of soothing sound that can help ease anxiety and create a serene atmosphere. For pets that are recovering from illness or surgery, ambient music can promote healing by reducing stress and encouraging restful sleep. This genre is also beneficial for animals that have experienced trauma or are adjusting to new environments, as it supports a calm, grounding energy.

While classical and ambient music are excellent choices for general calming, certain frequencies can be even more effective at targeting specific emotional and energetic issues. For instance, 432 Hz, often referred to as the "healing frequency," is thought to resonate with the heart, promoting feelings of peace and emotional stability. Many holistic practitioners believe that 432 Hz aligns with the natural frequency of the Earth, making it ideal for grounding pets and restoring energetic balance. Playing music tuned to this frequency can help soothe anxious or hyperactive animals and promote a sense of harmony within their environment.

Similarly, 528 Hz, sometimes called the "miracle tone," is associated with DNA repair and healing. This frequency is often used in sound therapy to promote physical and emotional recovery, making it an excellent choice for pets recovering from surgery, injury, or illness. Music tuned to 528 Hz can support the body's natural healing processes while providing emotional comfort and reducing stress. You can find specially composed tracks that use these healing frequencies, which can be played during rest or while administering other holistic treatments such as massage or Reiki.

While music therapy is primarily used for calming and emotional support, it can also be utilized to stimulate energy and encourage activity in lethargic or older pets. Upbeat, rhythmic music with a faster tempo can help elevate your pet's energy levels, making it ideal for playtime or exercise. Rhythmic drumming, for example, can stimulate physical activity and focus, making it useful for pets that need encouragement to move or engage. This type of music resonates with the Root and Solar Plexus Chakras, helping to activate physical vitality and personal power.

In addition to the music itself, certain instruments and sounds can have profound effects on your pet's energy. Instruments such as Tibetan singing bowls, gongs, and wind chimes produce resonant tones that can help clear energetic blockages and promote deep relaxation. These instruments work particularly well during holistic treatments like Reiki or meditation, as they create vibrations that synchronize with the body's natural energy flow.

Tibetan singing bowls, in particular, produce sound waves that can resonate with the body's chakras, helping to balance energy and reduce tension. When the bowl is played, the vibrations ripple through the space, affecting both the physical and energetic bodies. Pets often respond well to the soft, continuous tones of the bowls, which can help calm anxiety, clear mental fog, and promote overall balance. For animals that are nervous or highly sensitive, incorporating singing bowls into their daily routine can help create a soothing, stable environment that supports their emotional well-being.

Similarly, wind chimes or bells can produce soft, high-pitched sounds that cleanse the energy of a space and help dispel any negative or stagnant energy. Placing wind chimes in areas where your pet spends a lot of time—such as near their bed or in the backyard—can create a continuous flow of calming, uplifting energy. The gentle tinkling of the chimes helps to harmonize the environment and promote a sense of peace and safety.

When incorporating music therapy into your pet's holistic care routine, it's important to observe how they respond to different types of music and sounds. Each animal is unique, and what works for one pet may not necessarily have the same effect on another. Some animals may immediately relax in response to classical music, while others may prefer the softer, ambient sounds of nature recordings, such as rain or birdsong. Pay close attention to your pet's behavior—signs of relaxation, such as lying down, closing their eyes, or breathing deeply, indicate that the music is having a positive effect.

On the other hand, if your pet seems restless, agitated, or disinterested, it may be best to try a different type of music or adjust the volume. Keep the volume at a moderate level, as animals have more sensitive hearing than humans and may find loud or abrupt sounds stressful rather than soothing. The goal is to create an atmosphere that supports their emotional and energetic balance, so always allow your pet to guide the process with their reactions.

Music therapy can be incorporated into your pet's daily routine in various ways, from playing calming music during meal times to setting the tone for relaxation during car rides, vet visits, or other potentially stressful situations. It can also be used as part of a healing ritual or as background music during other holistic treatments like massage, Reiki, or aromatherapy. Over time, as your pet becomes familiar with certain types of music or sounds, they may come to associate these tones with feelings of safety, comfort, and relaxation, further enhancing the therapeutic effects.

Music therapy offers a powerful yet gentle way to support your pet's emotional and energetic well-being. By selecting calming or stimulating music, tuned frequencies, and healing instruments, you can influence your pet's energy field, reduce anxiety, and promote healing. Whether used daily to maintain balance or during specific situations that require extra emotional support, music therapy is a valuable addition to your holistic care toolkit, helping to create a more peaceful and harmonious environment for your pet. In the next chapter, we will explore more advanced techniques in music therapy, including the use of specific healing frequencies and their effects on balancing your pet's chakras and emotional state.

Building on the foundation of music therapy introduced in the previous chapter, this section delves deeper into the use of specific sound frequencies and their effects on the animal body, mind, and energy field. Sound therapy, when applied with intention, can have profound healing effects on pets, helping to balance their chakras, alleviate emotional and behavioral issues, and promote overall well-being. In this chapter, we will explore advanced techniques in music therapy, focusing on how healing frequencies, such as Solfeggio tones and binaural beats, can influence your pet's energy and support holistic healing.

Sound waves are essentially vibrations that interact with the body's energy field, resonating with different parts of the body depending on their frequency. In holistic healing, certain frequencies are believed to correspond with specific chakras or emotional states, allowing sound therapy to be targeted for precise energetic effects. By using healing frequencies intentionally, you can help unblock stagnant energy, harmonize the chakras, and provide emotional support for your pet.

One of the most well-known systems of healing frequencies is the Solfeggio scale, a set of ancient musical frequencies believed to promote healing and transformation. Each frequency in the Solfeggio scale is associated with a different aspect of physical, emotional, and spiritual health. While this system has traditionally been used in human sound therapy, animals can benefit from its effects as well, particularly in terms of chakra balancing and emotional healing.

The six main frequencies of the Solfeggio scale and their associated benefits are:

396 Hz: Known for its ability to release fear and guilt, 396 Hz is associated with the Root Chakra, which governs physical security, stability, and grounding. This frequency can be especially beneficial for pets that are anxious, fearful, or insecure, as it helps clear energy blockages in the Root Chakra and promotes a sense of safety and stability. Playing music tuned to 396 Hz can help reduce stress in pets, particularly during situations that trigger anxiety, such as vet visits, car rides, or thunderstorms.

417 Hz: This frequency is associated with the process of change and emotional release. It resonates with the Sacral Chakra, which governs emotions, creativity, and relationships. 417 Hz is particularly useful for pets that have experienced trauma, neglect, or emotional imbalance, as it helps clear stagnant energy in the Sacral Chakra and encourages emotional healing. If your pet is struggling with fear, anxiety, or behavioral issues related to past trauma, playing music at 417 Hz can support their emotional recovery.

528 Hz: Often referred to as the "miracle tone," 528 Hz is believed to promote transformation and healing at the cellular level. It is associated with the Solar Plexus Chakra, which governs personal power, confidence, and energy. Playing music at 528 Hz can help boost your pet's vitality and encourage emotional resilience, making it an excellent frequency for pets recovering from illness or injury. It also promotes harmony in relationships, making it beneficial for multi-pet households or pets that are adjusting to new family members.

639 Hz: This frequency resonates with the Heart Chakra, which governs love, compassion, and emotional balance. Music

tuned to 639 Hz is ideal for fostering connection between you and your pet, as it promotes emotional healing and the development of deep, trusting relationships. It's particularly useful for pets that are grieving, anxious, or withdrawn, as it helps open the Heart Chakra and restore emotional balance. Playing 639 Hz during bonding time or when your pet is resting can strengthen your connection and promote feelings of safety and love.

741 Hz: Known for its detoxifying and purifying effects, 741 Hz is associated with the Throat Chakra, which governs communication and self-expression. This frequency can help clear energetic blockages related to communication, making it beneficial for pets that have difficulty expressing their needs or emotions. Playing music at 741 Hz can also support physical detoxification, helping to cleanse the body of toxins and promote overall health.

852 Hz: This frequency resonates with the Third Eye Chakra, which governs intuition and mental clarity. Music tuned to 852 Hz can help calm an overactive mind and support intuitive perception, making it useful for pets that are highly sensitive or prone to stress. If your pet struggles with anxiety, nervousness, or confusion, playing 852 Hz can help bring mental clarity and emotional stability, promoting a deeper sense of calm.

Incorporating these Solfeggio frequencies into your pet's daily routine can be as simple as playing music tuned to these frequencies during rest, relaxation, or healing sessions. Many sound therapy tracks are available online, specifically designed to emit these frequencies, making it easy to integrate them into your pet's holistic care plan. Whether you're using them to calm an anxious pet, support emotional healing, or enhance the bond between you and your pet, these frequencies can help promote a deeper sense of harmony and well-being.

Another powerful sound therapy technique that can benefit pets is the use of binaural beats. Binaural beats are created by playing two slightly different frequencies in each ear, which the brain perceives as a single tone. This tone is believed to influence brainwave activity, promoting specific mental and emotional states depending on the frequency of the beats. While binaural beats are typically used with headphones, they can still be effective for pets when played through speakers, as the vibrational energy of the beats affects the brain and energy field even without direct ear stimulation.

Different binaural beat frequencies are associated with different states of consciousness:

Delta waves (1-4 Hz): These are the slowest brainwaves, associated with deep sleep and physical healing. Playing delta wave binaural beats can help pets relax into a deep, restorative sleep, making them ideal for pets recovering from surgery, injury, or illness. Delta waves also support the healing of the Root Chakra, promoting physical strength and stability.

Theta waves (4-8 Hz): Theta waves are associated with deep relaxation, meditation, and emotional healing. These frequencies are beneficial for pets that are anxious, stressed, or emotionally unsettled, as they promote a state of calm and balance. Theta waves can also help enhance the healing of the Heart and Solar Plexus Chakras, supporting emotional resilience and confidence.

Alpha waves (8-12 Hz): These brainwaves are linked to a relaxed yet alert state of mind, often experienced during light meditation or quiet focus. Alpha waves are useful for pets that need to stay calm but awake, such as during travel or periods of rest after physical activity. Alpha waves help balance the Throat and Third Eye Chakras, encouraging mental clarity and communication.

Beta waves (12-30 Hz): These are faster brainwaves, associated with focus, problem-solving, and active thinking. Beta waves can help energize pets that are lethargic or unfocused, promoting physical activity and engagement. Beta wave binaural beats can stimulate the Solar Plexus Chakra, helping pets feel more confident and energized.

By incorporating binaural beats into your pet's music therapy sessions, you can help guide their brainwaves toward a desired state—whether it's deep sleep, calm focus, or energetic activity. As with other sound therapy techniques, it's important to observe your pet's reactions to binaural beats and adjust the frequency and volume to their preferences. Some pets may respond more strongly to certain frequencies than others, so be mindful of their behavior and adjust the therapy as needed.

In addition to Solfeggio frequencies and binaural beats, natural soundscapes, such as rain, ocean waves, or birdsong, can also be effective in promoting relaxation and energetic balance. Many pets are soothed by the sounds of nature, which can mimic the environment of their ancestral habitats. Playing natural soundscapes in the background can help calm anxious or stressed pets, providing a comforting and familiar auditory environment that promotes emotional stability and peace.

Combining these advanced sound therapy techniques with other holistic treatments, such as Reiki, aromatherapy, or crystal healing, can create a multi-sensory healing experience that amplifies the effects of each modality. For example, playing Solfeggio frequencies during a Reiki session can enhance the flow of energy through the chakras, while using binaural beats alongside aromatherapy can deepen your pet's state of relaxation and promote emotional healing.

In conclusion, sound therapy offers a powerful and versatile tool for addressing your pet's emotional, physical, and energetic needs. By exploring healing frequencies, binaural beats, and natural soundscapes, you can create a personalized sound therapy routine that promotes balance, healing, and overall well-being for your pet. Whether you are helping your pet recover from illness, calm their anxiety, or simply maintain their emotional and energetic health, sound therapy provides a gentle and effective means of holistic healing. In the next chapter, we will explore breathing and meditation techniques that you can practice alongside your pet, further enhancing your bond and supporting their holistic well-being.

Chapter 10
Breathing and Meditation Techniques with Pets

Breathing and meditation are powerful tools that not only benefit humans but can also be incredibly effective in enhancing the well-being of pets. Animals are highly attuned to their environment and to the energy of the people they interact with, which means that their emotional and physical state is often influenced by the energy around them. In this chapter, we will explore how practicing mindful breathing and meditation alongside your pet can strengthen your bond, calm their nervous system, and support both their mental and physical health.

Breathing is fundamental to life, and the rhythm and depth of our breath have a profound effect on our emotional and physical state. This holds true for animals as well. Pets can mirror the stress or calmness of their owners, and by practicing deep, slow breathing with your pet, you can help regulate their nervous system and promote a state of calm. Conscious breathing is a simple but highly effective practice that can help relieve stress, anxiety, and tension in pets, especially those prone to nervousness or hyperactivity.

To begin incorporating breathing exercises into your pet's routine, find a quiet space where both you and your pet can relax comfortably. Sit next to your pet or hold them gently, depending on their size and comfort level. Begin by focusing on your own breath, inhaling deeply through your nose and exhaling slowly through your mouth. As you breathe, try to match the rhythm of your breath to a calming, steady pace. Your pet will begin to sense the shift in your energy and often, in response, their own breathing will start to slow down and become more regular.

You can enhance this breathing practice by using gentle touch, placing one hand on your pet's body—perhaps on their back, chest, or belly—wherever they feel comfortable. This light physical contact helps your pet feel secure and connected to you. As you breathe deeply and slowly, imagine that the calming energy of your breath is flowing through your hand into your pet, gently easing any stress or tension they might be holding. This not only calms their physical body but also soothes their emotional and energetic state.

For anxious pets, breathing exercises can be especially useful during stressful situations such as thunderstorms, fireworks, or vet visits. By practicing deep breathing regularly, you can teach your pet to associate this activity with relaxation, making it easier to calm them when needed. Over time, your pet will begin to recognize the shift in energy and will likely respond more quickly to the calming effect of your breath.

Another form of mindful practice that is deeply beneficial for pets is meditation. Animals are naturally intuitive and are able to pick up on the energy of meditation, which is calming and grounding. Meditating with your pet is an excellent way to foster a deep energetic connection, allowing both of you to enter a peaceful state of relaxation together. This practice not only helps soothe your pet but also enhances the emotional bond between you.

To begin a meditation session with your pet, find a quiet, comfortable space where your pet feels safe and secure. Sit or lie down in a relaxed position, allowing your pet to rest beside you. If your pet is small enough, you may hold them in your lap, but larger pets can simply sit next to you or lay at your feet. Close your eyes and take a few deep breaths to center yourself, focusing on releasing any tension or distractions.

As you enter a meditative state, focus on the feeling of peace and calm within yourself. Visualize this peaceful energy expanding from your body, enveloping both you and your pet in a cocoon of light and tranquility. You can imagine this light as a soft, soothing color—perhaps green for healing, blue for calm, or pink for love—and allow this energy to flow over and through both of you. Animals are highly responsive to energy, and many will sense this shift and begin to relax deeply in response.

While meditating, you may notice that your pet becomes calm and even sleepy. Some pets may settle into a peaceful state immediately, while others may need time to adjust to the energy of meditation. Be patient and let your pet find their own way into the practice. The goal is not to force them into stillness but to create an environment where they feel safe, relaxed, and connected to you.

Pets that are highly sensitive or anxious can especially benefit from the grounding effects of meditation. These animals often pick up on the emotional energy of their environment, making it difficult for them to find peace in a chaotic or stressful atmosphere. By meditating with your pet regularly, you create a consistent space of calm that they can rely on, helping to soothe their nervous system and promote emotional stability.

Meditation can also be used to support pets during times of healing or recovery. If your pet is recovering from surgery, illness, or injury, practicing meditation with them can help promote a sense of peace and relaxation, which is essential for the healing process. As you meditate, focus your intention on sending healing energy to your pet. Visualize their body bathed in a soft, golden light, filling every cell with warmth and vitality. Imagine this light restoring balance to their energy field, clearing any blockages, and promoting physical healing.

For older pets, meditation can help ease the discomfort that often comes with aging. As pets grow older, they may experience physical pain, stiffness, or emotional changes related to declining health. Meditation can provide a gentle, supportive space for them to relax, release tension, and feel comforted by your presence. Even short meditation sessions can have a profound effect on their well-being, promoting relaxation and emotional ease.

In addition to individual meditation sessions, guided meditations designed specifically for pets can be a useful tool. These guided sessions often incorporate calming music, gentle breathing cues, and visualization exercises that are tailored to pets and their energy needs. Playing a guided meditation in the background while you sit with your pet can help both of you relax into the experience and deepen the bond between you.

Another variation of meditation that can be highly effective for pets is walking meditation. This practice involves taking a slow, mindful walk with your pet, focusing on the present moment and the connection between you. During the walk, focus on each step you take, the feel of the ground beneath your feet, and the rhythm of your pet walking beside you. Allow the walk to become a meditative experience, where both you and your pet can connect with nature and each other. This type of meditation is particularly useful for dogs, as it provides them with physical activity while promoting mental and emotional balance.

Breathing and meditation, when practiced regularly with your pet, offer a simple yet profound way to promote holistic well-being. These practices not only help calm the mind and body but also strengthen the energetic connection between you and your pet. By dedicating time to mindfulness, you create a space of safety, peace, and love that benefits both of you on a deep, energetic level.

One of the most powerful techniques to incorporate into your meditation practice with pets is chakra-focused breathing and visualization. This method involves focusing on specific chakras in your pet's body, visualizing energy flowing through those chakras, and using your breath to guide and balance the energy. As you learned earlier in the book, animals have their own chakra system, which corresponds to different aspects of their physical, emotional, and spiritual well-being. By aligning your breathing and intention with the flow of energy through these chakras, you can help unblock stagnant energy, calm emotional distress, and promote healing.

To begin a chakra-focused meditation with your pet, start by finding a quiet, comfortable space where you can both relax. Have your pet lie down or sit next to you, and take a few moments to center yourself with deep, slow breathing. Once you feel grounded and calm, bring your attention to your pet's chakras, starting with the Root Chakra at the base of the spine. The Root Chakra governs physical stability, safety, and security, making it a key area to focus on for pets dealing with anxiety, fear, or insecurity.

As you breathe deeply, visualize a warm, red light surrounding your pet's Root Chakra. Imagine this red light as a grounding, stabilizing force that helps your pet feel safe and secure. With each inhale, picture this energy growing stronger, and with each exhale, imagine any fear or anxiety being released from your pet's body. You can place one hand gently near the base of your pet's spine, allowing the energy to flow through your hand and into their Root Chakra.

Continue moving up through your pet's body, focusing on the Sacral Chakra (located just below the belly), the Solar Plexus Chakra (just below the ribcage), the Heart Chakra (in the chest), the Throat Chakra (in the neck), the Third Eye Chakra (between the eyes), and finally the Crown Chakra (at the top of the head). For each chakra, visualize the corresponding color—orange for the Sacral Chakra, yellow for the Solar Plexus, green for the Heart, blue for the Throat, indigo for the Third Eye, and violet for the Crown. Imagine the light of each chakra becoming brighter and more balanced with each breath, and feel your connection with your pet deepen as you guide their energy into harmony.

Another technique that can enhance your chakra meditation is healing breathwork, or pranic breathing, which involves using your breath to channel energy directly to your pet. Prana, or life force energy, is the subtle energy that flows through all living beings, and by consciously directing prana through your breath, you can help strengthen your pet's energy field. This practice is particularly useful for pets that are recovering from illness or injury, as it promotes healing and replenishes depleted energy.

To practice pranic breathing, begin by sitting comfortably with your pet in front of you. Take a deep breath in, imagining that you are drawing in pure, healing energy from the universe.

As you exhale, visualize this energy flowing from your heart or hands into your pet's body. Focus on any areas where your pet may need healing, such as a specific injury or chakra that feels out of balance. As you continue breathing, imagine the energy filling your pet's body, revitalizing their cells and restoring balance to their energy field.

You can combine this pranic breathwork with visualization for an even more powerful effect. For example, if your pet has an injury, visualize the healing energy entering the injured area as a warm, golden light that repairs and strengthens the tissues. With each breath, see the injury becoming smaller and less inflamed, until it is fully healed. If your pet is emotionally distressed, focus on their Heart Chakra, sending love and calming energy through your breath, and imagine their emotional wounds being soothed and healed.

For pets that are particularly sensitive or highly energetic, guided meditation and healing visualizations can help calm their nervous system and promote emotional stability. These visualizations work by focusing your mind on specific calming images or symbols that resonate with your pet's energy, helping them to relax and release stress. For example, if your pet is anxious or hyperactive, you can guide them through a visualization of a peaceful, calming scene—such as a meadow, beach, or forest—where they feel safe and relaxed.

To practice this with your pet, find a quiet space and sit or lie down together. Close your eyes and begin by focusing on your breath, then visualize your pet in a peaceful setting. You can imagine them lying in a field of soft grass, with the warmth of the sun on their fur and a gentle breeze flowing around them. Picture your pet's body becoming more relaxed as they breathe in the fresh air, and see any tension or anxiety slowly dissipating into the earth. As you hold this image in your mind, you may find that your pet starts to relax in response, as they naturally attune to the peaceful energy of your visualization.

If your pet struggles with fear or insecurity, you can guide them through a visualization that focuses on grounding and protection. Imagine your pet surrounded by a protective circle of light, which keeps them safe from harm and helps them feel secure. Visualize this light as a shield that protects them from external stressors, such as loud noises, unfamiliar people, or other animals. You can also incorporate this visualization into your daily routine, imagining the protective light surrounding your pet whenever they are in a potentially stressful situation, such as during a trip to the vet or while traveling.

In addition to these practices, healing mantras or sounds can also be incorporated into your meditation sessions to help balance your pet's energy. Certain sounds and mantras, when repeated during meditation, can have a calming and harmonizing effect on the body's energy centers. The mantra "Om," for instance, is considered a universal sound of creation and connection, and chanting this mantra during meditation can help align both you and your pet's energy fields with the vibrations of the universe.

To use mantras in your meditation practice with your pet, sit quietly with your pet and begin chanting the chosen mantra in a soft, rhythmic tone. As you chant, visualize the sound waves vibrating through your pet's body, harmonizing their energy and calming their nervous system. You may notice that your pet responds to the soothing vibration of the sound by relaxing or even falling asleep. Mantras can be used during meditation sessions focused on specific chakras, with different sounds corresponding to each chakra. For example, the sound "Lam" is associated with the Root Chakra, "Vam" with the Sacral Chakra, and so on. Repeating these sounds can help balance the corresponding chakras in your pet's body, promoting overall energetic harmony.

These advanced breathing and meditation techniques can be practiced regularly to maintain your pet's energetic health, or used as needed during times of stress, illness, or emotional difficulty. The key to success with these practices is consistency and patience—by making these techniques a regular part of your routine, you will help create a calm, balanced environment in which your pet can thrive.

It's important to remember that, just as with humans, every pet is unique and may respond differently to various meditation and energy techniques. Some pets may be more receptive to visualization, while others respond better to breathwork or sound healing. Take the time to observe your pet's reactions and adjust your practice accordingly, tailoring each session to meet their specific needs.

In summary, these advanced breathing and meditation techniques offer a powerful way to support your pet's emotional and energetic well-being. By focusing on chakra balancing, pranic breathing, healing visualizations, and sound work, you can help restore harmony to your pet's energy field, promote healing, and deepen your bond. In the next chapter, we will explore phytotherapy, focusing on how medicinal plants and herbs can be used to support your pet's health and well-being in a natural, holistic way.

Chapter 11
Using Medicinal Plants

Phytotherapy, the use of medicinal plants and herbs for healing, has been practiced for centuries and is an integral part of holistic medicine. For animals, phytotherapy offers a natural and gentle way to support health, alleviate ailments, and promote balance in both the body and mind. Just like humans, pets can benefit from the healing properties of certain herbs, which can be used to treat various conditions, boost the immune system, and improve overall well-being. This chapter introduces the reader to phytotherapy for pets, focusing on safe and effective plants that can be used to support their health naturally.

When using phytotherapy with animals, it's essential to understand that not all herbs are safe for pets. Some plants that are beneficial for humans can be toxic to animals, so it's important to be well-informed and consult with a holistic veterinarian before introducing new herbs into your pet's routine. With the proper knowledge, however, medicinal plants can be a powerful addition to your pet's holistic care plan, helping to treat conditions such as anxiety, digestive issues, inflammation, and skin problems.

One of the most widely used medicinal herbs in animal phytotherapy is chamomile (Matricaria chamomilla). Chamomile is known for its calming and anti-inflammatory properties, making it an excellent herb for pets dealing with stress, anxiety, or digestive upset. Chamomile can be given to pets as a tea, added to their water, or applied topically to soothe skin irritations. Its gentle nature makes it especially useful for calming anxious pets during stressful situations such as vet visits, thunderstorms, or car rides.

Chamomile is also beneficial for pets with gastrointestinal issues, as it helps soothe the digestive tract and reduce inflammation. For dogs or cats that experience frequent stomach upset, bloating, or gas, chamomile tea can be administered in small amounts to promote digestive balance. Additionally, its mild sedative effects make chamomile useful for pets that have difficulty relaxing or sleeping. A chamomile infusion given before bedtime can help ease them into a restful sleep, especially if they are recovering from illness or injury.

Another powerful herb in animal phytotherapy is calendula (Calendula officinalis), also known as marigold. Calendula is highly regarded for its skin-healing properties and is often used to treat wounds, burns, rashes, and other skin irritations. It has anti-inflammatory, antifungal, and antibacterial properties, making it a versatile herb for treating various skin conditions in pets. Calendula can be applied topically as a cream, salve, or infused oil to promote wound healing and soothe itchy or irritated skin.

For pets with chronic skin conditions such as dermatitis or hot spots, calendula can help reduce inflammation and promote faster healing. It can also be used to treat minor cuts, scrapes, or insect bites. In addition to its topical uses, calendula has internal benefits as well—it can help support the lymphatic system, boost the immune system, and promote overall detoxification. Calendula tea or tincture, when given in small, safe doses, can be used to support your pet's immune health and help clear out toxins from their body.

Valerian root (Valeriana officinalis) is another herb commonly used in phytotherapy for its calming and sedative properties. Valerian is particularly beneficial for pets that suffer from anxiety, hyperactivity, or nervousness. Unlike chamomile, valerian has a more potent sedative effect, making it useful for pets that have a higher level of anxiety or agitation. Valerian can be administered as a tincture, capsule, or tea, depending on the pet's size and tolerance.

For pets that become overly anxious during thunderstorms, fireworks, or separation, valerian can help calm their nerves and reduce symptoms of stress. Its calming effect also makes valerian useful for pets with behavioral issues related to anxiety, such as excessive barking, pacing, or destructive behavior. However, because valerian is quite strong, it should be used in moderation and only for short periods to avoid dependency or over-sedation.

Peppermint (Mentha piperita) is another popular herb in phytotherapy that offers multiple benefits for animals. Known for its cooling, anti-inflammatory, and digestive properties, peppermint is often used to alleviate digestive issues such as nausea, gas, and bloating. Peppermint can be brewed into a tea and given in small amounts to help soothe an upset stomach or digestive discomfort in pets. It is particularly helpful for dogs and cats that experience motion sickness or gastrointestinal issues during travel.

Topically, peppermint oil can be used to cool and soothe inflamed muscles or joints in pets suffering from arthritis or other inflammatory conditions. However, peppermint oil should always be diluted before applying to a pet's skin, as it is highly concentrated and can cause irritation if used undiluted. Additionally, care should be taken to avoid using peppermint oil around the nose and mouth of pets, as its strong scent can be overwhelming for animals.

For respiratory support, thyme (Thymus vulgaris) is an excellent herb for pets with colds, coughs, or respiratory infections. Thyme has natural antimicrobial and expectorant properties, making it useful for clearing mucus and soothing the respiratory tract. Thyme tea or a diluted thyme tincture can be administered to pets experiencing coughs or congestion, helping to clear their airways and boost their immune system.

Thyme can also be beneficial for pets with bacterial or fungal infections, as it has strong antimicrobial properties. For topical use, thyme can be brewed into a tea and used as a wash for fungal infections or skin irritations. However, as with all herbs, it's important to ensure that thyme is used in the appropriate dosage for pets, as excessive amounts can cause digestive upset.

Another herb commonly used in animal phytotherapy is milk thistle (Silybum marianum), which is well-known for its liver-supporting properties. Milk thistle helps detoxify the liver and can be used to support pets with liver disease, exposure to toxins, or after a course of medication. The active compound in milk thistle, silymarin, protects liver cells from damage and supports the regeneration of healthy liver tissue.

Milk thistle is often used as a supplement for pets recovering from illness, as it aids in detoxification and promotes overall liver health. It is particularly beneficial for older pets or those that have been on long-term medications, as it helps to clear toxins from the body and reduce the burden on the liver. Milk thistle can be administered as a tincture, capsule, or powder mixed into food.

For immune support and overall vitality, echinacea (Echinacea purpurea) is a powerful herb used in both human and animal phytotherapy. Echinacea is known for its ability to boost the immune system and fight off infections, making it useful for pets that are prone to colds, respiratory infections, or other immune-related issues. It can be used preventatively during times of stress or illness to strengthen the immune response and help the body fight off pathogens.

Echinacea can be given to pets as a tea, tincture, or capsule, depending on the pet's size and condition. When used properly, echinacea helps to shorten the duration of infections and promotes faster recovery. It is particularly useful during seasonal changes when pets are more susceptible to illnesses or when they are exposed to environments where they might catch colds, such as boarding facilities or kennels.

Lastly, ginger (Zingiber officinale) is an excellent herb for pets experiencing nausea, motion sickness, or digestive upset. Ginger is a natural anti-inflammatory and digestive aid, helping to soothe the stomach, reduce nausea, and alleviate gas and bloating. For pets that experience car sickness, ginger can be given as a small piece of raw root or brewed into a tea before travel to help prevent nausea and vomiting.

Ginger also has anti-inflammatory properties that make it useful for pets with joint pain or arthritis. When given in small amounts, ginger can help reduce inflammation and improve mobility in pets with chronic pain. However, ginger should always be administered in moderation, as excessive amounts can cause digestive upset.

Incorporating phytotherapy into your pet's holistic care routine offers a natural, gentle way to support their health and well-being. Whether used to calm anxiety, soothe digestive issues, promote healing, or boost the immune system, medicinal herbs provide a valuable tool for addressing a wide range of health concerns in pets. In the next chapter, we will explore more advanced applications of phytotherapy, focusing on how to create personalized herbal blends for specific conditions, as well as safe methods for administering herbs through infusions, tinctures, and oils.

Building upon the foundational knowledge of safe herbs for pets, this chapter delves into advanced applications of phytotherapy, exploring how to create personalized herbal blends for specific conditions, and the various methods of administering herbs, including infusions, tinctures, and essential oils. With the proper knowledge and care, you can use medicinal plants to tailor treatments to your pet's unique health needs, whether they are facing chronic conditions like arthritis, stress, or allergies, or simply need an immune boost to stay vibrant and healthy.

One of the most effective ways to harness the power of herbs for pets is by creating personalized herbal blends. This allows you to combine different herbs that address multiple aspects of your pet's health, enhancing the overall therapeutic effect. For example, a pet suffering from anxiety and digestive upset may benefit from a blend of calming herbs, such as chamomile and valerian, alongside digestive-supporting herbs like peppermint or ginger. Blending herbs allows you to create a more holistic treatment that addresses both emotional and physical symptoms simultaneously.

When creating herbal blends, it's important to consider the individual needs of your pet and choose herbs that complement one another. Start by identifying the primary health issue or imbalance, such as stress, inflammation, or digestive upset. Then, choose a few herbs that target this primary issue while also supporting secondary aspects of their health, such as boosting the immune system or promoting relaxation. As with any treatment, always consult with a holistic veterinarian to ensure that the herbs you choose are safe and appropriate for your pet's species, size, and health condition.

For example, if you have a dog that suffers from chronic arthritis, you might create an herbal blend that includes turmeric (Curcuma longa) for its powerful anti-inflammatory effects, ginger for its ability to reduce joint pain and support digestion, and devil's claw (Harpagophytum procumbens), another anti-inflammatory herb known for its pain-relieving properties. By combining these herbs, you can create a more effective remedy that targets both pain and inflammation, while also supporting the digestive system, which is often affected by chronic conditions.

For pets experiencing chronic stress or anxiety, a calming blend could include chamomile, valerian, and passionflower (Passiflora incarnata). Chamomile provides gentle relaxation, valerian helps with more intense nervousness, and passionflower promotes overall emotional balance and relaxation. This combination can help your pet feel calmer in stressful situations, such as during travel, loud noises, or periods of separation.

Once you have chosen the appropriate herbs for your pet's needs, you'll need to decide how to administer them. There are several methods for giving herbs to pets, each with its own advantages depending on the condition being treated and the pet's temperament.

One of the simplest and most commonly used methods is the herbal infusion. An infusion is essentially a strong herbal tea, made by steeping dried or fresh herbs in hot water to extract their medicinal properties. This method is ideal for gentle, internal use, especially for digestive or calming herbs. Infusions can be mixed into your pet's water, food, or given directly in small doses using a dropper or syringe.

To make an herbal infusion for your pet, start by boiling water and pouring it over the selected herbs. For smaller animals, you'll only need about a teaspoon of dried herbs per cup of water; for larger animals, you can increase the quantity to a tablespoon. Allow the herbs to steep for 10 to 15 minutes, then strain the liquid and let it cool to room temperature before administering. Be sure to give the infusion in small, measured doses based on your pet's size and the strength of the herbs.

For example, if your pet is experiencing an upset stomach, you can prepare a simple infusion using peppermint or ginger. These herbs help to soothe digestive discomfort, reduce gas, and alleviate nausea. For anxious pets, an infusion made with chamomile or lemon balm can provide gentle relaxation and help calm their nerves.

Another common method for administering herbs to pets is through tinctures. Tinctures are liquid extracts of herbs, usually made by soaking the herbs in alcohol or glycerin to concentrate their medicinal properties. Tinctures are highly potent and are typically given in very small amounts, making them ideal for pets that are resistant to taking larger volumes of herbal infusions or capsules.

For pets, it is important to use glycerin-based tinctures, as alcohol-based tinctures can be too harsh for animals' sensitive systems. Glycerin-based tinctures are gentler and more palatable, and can be added to food, water, or given directly with a dropper. You can find pre-made glycerin tinctures for pets at many natural health stores, or you can make your own by soaking dried herbs in glycerin for several weeks.

Tinctures are especially useful for treating chronic conditions like joint pain, inflammation, or immune deficiencies. For example, a milk thistle tincture can be given to pets with liver disease or pets that need detoxification after a course of medication. Milk thistle helps to protect and regenerate liver cells, making it a valuable herb for supporting liver health. Similarly, a turmeric tincture can be used to reduce inflammation and pain in pets with arthritis or other inflammatory conditions.

For skin issues, such as rashes, wounds, or infections, topical herbal applications are highly effective. Herbs like calendula, comfrey, and goldenseal can be made into salves, creams, or oils to promote healing, reduce inflammation, and prevent infection. Calendula oil, for example, is a soothing and antibacterial remedy that can be applied to cuts, scrapes, or hot spots to speed up healing and reduce irritation.

To make a herbal salve, you'll need dried herbs and a carrier oil like olive oil, coconut oil, or jojoba oil. Start by gently heating the oil in a double boiler and adding the herbs, allowing them to steep in the oil over low heat for several hours. Once the herbs have infused the oil, strain the mixture and add beeswax to create a salve-like consistency. You can store the salve in a jar and apply it directly to your pet's skin as needed.

For pets with allergies or skin sensitivities, a calendula and comfrey salve can help soothe itching and reduce inflammation. Calendula's antibacterial properties protect against infection, while comfrey promotes tissue repair and speeds up the healing process. This type of salve is gentle enough to use on irritated skin and can be applied several times a day as needed.

In addition to infusions, tinctures, and salves, essential oils derived from medicinal plants offer another powerful way to support your pet's health, but they must be used with caution. Essential oils are highly concentrated and can be toxic to pets if used improperly. It's crucial to always dilute essential oils with a carrier oil before applying them to your pet's skin, and never allow your pet to ingest essential oils. Some oils, like tea tree and eucalyptus, should be avoided entirely, as they can cause adverse reactions in pets.

When using essential oils for pets, opt for gentle, pet-safe oils like lavender, chamomile, and frankincense, which can be diluted and applied topically or used in a diffuser. Lavender oil, for instance, is well-known for its calming effects and can be used to reduce anxiety and promote relaxation in pets. Diluted lavender oil can be applied to your pet's bedding, or a few drops can be added to a diffuser to create a calming atmosphere.

Frankincense oil is another excellent choice for promoting healing and reducing inflammation. It can be diluted with a carrier oil and applied to areas of joint pain or inflammation to support mobility and comfort in pets with arthritis. However, always start with a very small amount, and observe your pet's reaction to ensure they are comfortable with the scent and application.

When creating personalized herbal remedies for your pet, it's important to monitor their response to the treatment closely. Every animal is different, and while one pet may respond well to a particular herb or blend, another may need adjustments to the dosage or type of herb. Always introduce new herbs slowly, starting with small doses, and watch for any signs of discomfort, allergic reactions, or digestive upset.

Incorporating phytotherapy into your pet's holistic care routine allows you to harness the healing power of nature to support their well-being in a gentle and natural way. Whether you are using herbs to calm anxiety, boost the immune system, treat chronic pain, or support recovery from illness, phytotherapy offers a wide range of solutions for promoting health and balance in your pet's life.

In the next chapter, we will explore Bach Flower Remedies and other vibrational essences, focusing on how these natural remedies can be used to balance your pet's emotional state and address behavioral issues such as fear, aggression, or anxiety. These subtle, energetic treatments offer another layer of holistic support, helping to restore emotional and energetic harmony in your pet's life.

Chapter 12
Bach Flower Remedies and Other Vibrational Essences

Bach Flower Remedies, developed by Dr. Edward Bach in the 1930s, are a form of vibrational medicine that address emotional imbalances by using the healing properties of flowers. These remedies are particularly well-suited for pets, as they work gently on the emotional and energetic levels to harmonize mood and behavior without causing side effects or interfering with other treatments. In addition to Bach Flower Remedies, other vibrational essences such as gem and environmental essences can also be used to help restore balance to your pet's emotional state. In this chapter, we will explore the use of Bach Flower Remedies to treat common emotional and behavioral problems in pets, focusing on their gentle yet profound ability to address fear, anxiety, aggression, and more.

Animals, like humans, experience a wide range of emotions that can manifest as behavioral problems when they are out of balance. Pets may experience fear, anxiety, aggression, loneliness, or even depression as a result of changes in their environment, traumatic experiences, or emotional sensitivity. Bach Flower Remedies provide a gentle way to restore emotional equilibrium by targeting the root cause of the emotional imbalance rather than just the symptoms.

The Bach Flower system consists of 38 different remedies, each derived from flowers and designed to address a specific emotional state. These remedies can be used individually or in combination, depending on the unique needs of your pet. They work by subtly shifting the animal's energy field, helping to clear emotional blockages and restore a sense of calm, security, and well-being.

One of the most commonly used remedies for pets is Rescue Remedy, a blend of five Bach Flower Remedies that is specifically designed for situations of acute stress or trauma. Rescue Remedy contains Star of Bethlehem (for shock and trauma), Rock Rose (for terror and panic), Impatiens (for stress and impatience), Cherry Plum (for loss of control), and Clematis (for grounding). This combination is particularly useful for pets that are experiencing immediate stress, such as during thunderstorms, fireworks, vet visits, or after an accident. Rescue Remedy can be given directly to the pet by adding a few drops to their water, food, or directly into their mouth. It is also available as a spray, which can be misted onto their fur or bedding.

For pets that suffer from chronic anxiety, Mimulus is a Bach Flower Remedy that addresses fear of known things, such as loud noises, strangers, or other animals. Mimulus is particularly helpful for shy or timid pets that are easily frightened by specific triggers. Pets that hide during thunderstorms, bark excessively when visitors arrive, or become anxious in new environments can benefit from Mimulus. By using this remedy consistently, you can help your pet build emotional resilience and reduce their sensitivity to external stressors.

Aspen is another remedy that is effective for treating general anxiety or fear of the unknown. Unlike Mimulus, which targets specific fears, Aspen is used when the pet is anxious but the cause is unclear. Pets that seem generally nervous, restless, or afraid without an obvious trigger may benefit from Aspen, as it helps alleviate vague or undefined fears. This remedy is especially useful for pets that exhibit nervous behaviors such as pacing, whining, or excessive grooming when there is no apparent reason for their distress.

For pets that have experienced trauma or abuse, Star of Bethlehem is a powerful remedy for emotional healing. This remedy helps to comfort and soothe pets that are recovering from past traumas, whether physical or emotional. It can be used for pets that were rescued from abusive situations or those that have undergone a sudden and traumatic event, such as being injured or abandoned. Star of Bethlehem helps the pet process and release the emotional pain associated with the trauma, allowing them to move forward and heal.

Rock Rose is another remedy that addresses acute fear and panic, particularly in situations where the pet is paralyzed by terror. This remedy is ideal for pets that go into a state of shock or freeze in response to a frightening situation. It is also helpful for pets that experience extreme fear during events like fireworks or thunderstorms, where they may become so terrified that they hide or refuse to move. Rock Rose helps to calm the pet's panic response, restoring a sense of peace and safety.

For pets that display aggressive behavior, Holly is a remedy that can help ease feelings of anger, jealousy, or resentment. Aggression in pets can stem from underlying emotional issues, such as feeling threatened, insecure, or territorial. Holly works by addressing the root cause of the aggression, helping the pet feel more secure and reducing their need to react defensively. It can be particularly useful for multi-pet households where one pet feels jealous or competitive with another, or for pets that exhibit aggression toward strangers or other animals.

Vervain is another remedy that can be helpful for pets that are hyperactive or overly excited. Pets that are constantly in a heightened state of excitement, whether from overstimulation or nervous energy, can benefit from Vervain's calming effects. This remedy helps the pet relax and maintain a balanced level of energy, making it ideal for pets that are easily excitable or that have difficulty calming down after playtime or exercise.

For pets that struggle with loneliness or separation anxiety, Heather and Chicory are two remedies that can provide emotional comfort. Heather is used for pets that seek constant attention and feel insecure when left alone. These pets may follow their owner from room to room or become anxious when they are not the center of attention. Heather helps them feel more secure in their own company and reduces their need for constant reassurance. Chicory, on the other hand, is used for pets that are overly possessive and demanding of attention. It helps these pets develop a healthier, more balanced attachment to their owner.

For older pets or those that seem to have lost interest in life, Wild Rose can be an effective remedy. Pets that are apathetic, listless, or appear to have given up on life can benefit from Wild Rose, as it helps restore their enthusiasm and zest for life. This remedy is especially useful for aging pets that have become disengaged or depressed due to health problems or loss of mobility. It helps rekindle their interest in their surroundings and brings a renewed sense of vitality.

When using Bach Flower Remedies, it's important to administer them consistently for the best results. While Rescue Remedy can be used in acute situations, other remedies may take time to work as they gently shift the pet's emotional energy. Remedies can be given directly in the pet's mouth, added to their water, or mixed into their food. You can also apply the remedies topically by rubbing a few drops onto the pet's fur, nose, or paws.

In addition to Bach Flower Remedies, other vibrational essences such as gem essences or environmental essences can be used to support emotional balance in pets. Gem essences, made by infusing gemstones in water, carry the energetic properties of the stones and can be used to address specific emotional or energetic imbalances. For example, a rose quartz essence can help promote love and emotional healing, while an amethyst essence can help calm the mind and reduce anxiety.

Environmental essences, made from natural elements like sunlight, moonlight, or specific locations, can also have a balancing effect on pets. These essences capture the energy of the environment and can be used to help pets that are sensitive to changes in their surroundings or that are adjusting to a new home or family dynamic.

When choosing vibrational essences, it's important to observe your pet's behavior and emotional state, selecting remedies that correspond to their specific needs. Just as with Bach Flower Remedies, vibrational essences work gently and are safe for long-term use, making them a valuable addition to your pet's holistic care routine.

Bach Flower Remedies and other vibrational essences provide a subtle yet powerful way to support your pet's emotional well-being. Whether your pet is dealing with fear, anxiety, aggression, or trauma, these remedies offer a gentle path to emotional balance and harmony. In the next chapter, we will explore how to deepen the use of these remedies by combining them to address more complex energetic imbalances, helping you create a personalized approach to restoring your pet's emotional health.

Building on the introduction to Bach Flower Remedies and other vibrational essences, this chapter explores the deepening of their use by combining remedies to address more complex emotional and energetic imbalances in pets. While single remedies can be effective for treating specific emotional states, many pets may experience overlapping issues—such as fear and aggression, or anxiety and attachment issues—requiring a more customized approach. By combining several remedies, you can create a holistic treatment plan that supports your pet's emotional well-being on multiple levels.

Combining Bach Flower Remedies is a straightforward process, and it allows you to tailor treatments to your pet's unique emotional landscape. Up to six or seven different remedies can be mixed together to form a personalized blend. This is particularly useful when your pet is exhibiting a range of emotional or behavioral issues that stem from different underlying causes. For example, a rescue dog may show signs of fear, anxiety, and mistrust, but also display aggressive tendencies when feeling threatened. A combination of remedies can address each of these aspects simultaneously, helping the pet heal in a more comprehensive way.

When creating a custom blend, start by identifying the most prominent issues affecting your pet. It's helpful to observe your pet's behavior over a period of time to understand the emotional patterns at play. If your pet is reactive, for example, consider whether the reactivity stems from fear, insecurity, territoriality, or frustration. Once you have a clearer picture, you can choose the remedies that address both the surface behaviors and the underlying emotional drivers.

For pets that have been rescued from difficult or traumatic situations, a combination of remedies can help them release the emotional scars from their past and adjust to their new environment. A useful blend might include Star of Bethlehem for healing trauma, Mimulus for fear of known things, and Walnut for adjusting to change. Star of Bethlehem comforts the pet, helping them process and release the emotional pain from their past. Mimulus addresses the specific fears the pet may have, such as fear of people or other animals, and Walnut helps them adapt to their new life and surroundings, easing the transition.

If the rescued pet also displays aggressive behavior as a defense mechanism, adding Holly to the blend can help ease feelings of anger, jealousy, or territoriality. In cases where the aggression is tied to a sense of insecurity or fear, Rock Rose may be more appropriate, as it addresses terror and panic, calming the pet's fight-or-flight response. This type of blend helps soothe the pet's nervous system, allowing them to feel more secure and less reactive to perceived threats.

For pets with separation anxiety, a combination of remedies can target both the emotional distress of being left alone and the behavioral manifestations of anxiety, such as destructive behavior, whining, or restlessness. Heather, Chicory, and Rescue Remedy are a powerful trio for these situations. Heather helps pets that seek constant attention and cannot bear being left alone, Chicory addresses possessiveness and excessive attachment, and Rescue Remedy provides immediate relief for acute anxiety or stress.

If the pet's separation anxiety is compounded by fear of abandonment, adding Mimulus or Aspen can further support emotional healing. Mimulus is helpful for pets that fear being abandoned or left behind, while Aspen addresses general unease and anxiety when the pet is alone, even if there is no obvious reason for their fear. This blend not only calms the immediate symptoms of separation anxiety but also works on deeper emotional levels to promote trust and security.

For pets that experience extreme anxiety during loud events—such as thunderstorms, fireworks, or travel—a combination of Rock Rose, Mimulus, and Rescue Remedy can be very effective. Rock Rose addresses terror and panic, Mimulus targets specific fears, and Rescue Remedy provides an overall calming effect in the face of acute stress. This blend can be given before, during, and after the event to help the pet remain calm and recover quickly from the stress.

Pets that are prone to obsessive behaviors, such as excessive grooming, chewing, or pacing, can benefit from a blend that includes Vervain and Beech. Vervain helps calm hyperactivity and restlessness, while Beech is useful for pets that exhibit rigid, compulsive behaviors or are overly sensitive to their environment. Adding Chestnut Bud to this blend can help pets break the cycle of repetitive behaviors by promoting learning and adaptation.

For pets with behavioral issues related to territoriality or dominance, a combination of Vine, Holly, and Walnut can be useful. Vine helps reduce the need for control and dominance, while Holly soothes feelings of jealousy or rivalry. Walnut aids in adapting to changes in the household, such as the introduction of a new pet or family member, which may trigger territorial behavior. Together, these remedies promote a more balanced, harmonious dynamic within the home, helping pets feel secure without the need to assert dominance or control.

Once you have selected the appropriate remedies, you can mix them together in a treatment bottle. To make a treatment bottle, combine two drops of each selected remedy into a small dropper bottle filled with spring water. This blend can be administered directly into your pet's mouth, added to their water or food, or applied topically to areas such as the ears, paws, or fur. Typically, four drops of the blend are given several times a day, depending on the severity of the emotional imbalance.

In addition to Bach Flower Remedies, other vibrational essences—such as gem or environmental essences—can be combined into these blends to provide an even more comprehensive approach to emotional healing. Gem essences, in particular, carry the energetic properties of healing stones and can be used to address specific emotional or energetic imbalances. For example, rose quartz essence promotes love, emotional healing, and trust, making it a useful addition to a blend for pets recovering from trauma or dealing with emotional insecurity.

Amethyst essence is known for its calming and soothing properties and can be added to blends for anxious or restless pets. This essence helps promote clarity, calmness, and emotional balance, supporting pets that are prone to stress or over-excitement. Clear quartz essence, on the other hand, is an all-purpose essence that amplifies the healing properties of other remedies, making it an excellent addition to any blend where you want to strengthen the overall energetic impact.

Environmental essences, such as those made from specific locations or natural phenomena, can also be incorporated into blends to support pets that are highly sensitive to their surroundings. For example, an essence made from the energy of a peaceful forest can help ground pets that are easily overstimulated by their environment, while a full moon essence can promote emotional release and renewal, making it helpful for pets processing trauma or grief.

When using a combination of Bach Flower Remedies and vibrational essences, the key is to observe your pet's response over time. Some emotional imbalances may resolve quickly, while others may take longer to heal as deeper layers of emotion are addressed. Patience and consistency are essential, and remedies can be adjusted as needed based on changes in your pet's behavior and emotional state.

It's also important to remember that vibrational essences work subtly, gently shifting the pet's energy over time. While they do not directly alter behavior in the way that training or other behavioral interventions might, they provide the energetic support needed to help the pet overcome emotional obstacles and restore balance. When used in conjunction with positive reinforcement and a nurturing environment, these remedies can play a significant role in your pet's emotional healing journey.

In conclusion, combining Bach Flower Remedies and other vibrational essences offers a powerful and customizable approach to addressing your pet's emotional and energetic needs. By creating personalized blends, you can provide holistic support for a wide range of issues, from fear and anxiety to aggression and trauma recovery. These remedies work gently and naturally, helping to restore harmony to your pet's emotional landscape. In the next chapter, we will explore how to balance the Root Chakra in pets, which is essential for promoting a sense of security, stability, and grounding in their lives.

Chapter 13
Balancing Animal Chakras
Focus on the Root Chakra

The Root Chakra, located at the base of the spine, is the foundation of the chakra system in animals, just as it is in humans. This energy center governs feelings of security, stability, grounding, and connection to the physical world. For animals, the Root Chakra is essential for establishing a sense of safety in their environment. When this chakra is balanced, pets feel confident, secure, and at ease in their surroundings. However, when it is blocked or unbalanced, pets may exhibit behaviors such as fear, anxiety, territorial aggression, or excessive shyness.

The Root Chakra is associated with the color red and the element of earth. This connection to the earth provides a grounding influence that helps animals feel stable and rooted, especially when they are exposed to new or stressful situations. Pets with a balanced Root Chakra tend to adapt more easily to changes in their environment, such as moving to a new home, meeting new people, or adjusting to other pets in the household. On the other hand, an imbalanced Root Chakra can lead to feelings of insecurity, causing pets to become anxious, defensive, or withdrawn.

One of the most common signs of an imbalanced Root Chakra in pets is anxiety, especially in situations where they feel unsafe or insecure. Pets with Root Chakra imbalances may react fearfully to loud noises, unfamiliar people, or new environments. They may exhibit nervous behaviors like pacing, excessive barking, or hiding. In some cases, pets may become overly attached to their owners, seeking constant reassurance and attention as a way to feel more grounded.

Another symptom of a blocked Root Chakra is territorial behavior. Pets that are overly protective of their space or belongings may be compensating for a lack of security in their environment. This can manifest as aggression toward other animals or humans, as the pet tries to assert control over their surroundings. In extreme cases, pets with territorial imbalances may become aggressive even toward family members or familiar pets, perceiving them as threats to their personal safety.

To restore balance to the Root Chakra, there are several holistic techniques you can use to help your pet feel more grounded and secure. One of the most effective methods is grounding through nature. Since the Root Chakra is associated with the earth element, spending time outdoors and allowing your pet to connect with nature is a powerful way to restore balance. Regular walks, playtime in the yard, or simply lying in the grass can help your pet release built-up stress and reconnect with the earth's stabilizing energy. For pets that live primarily indoors, bringing natural elements into their environment—such as plants, stones, or grounding crystals—can help mimic the calming effects of nature.

Another useful practice for balancing the Root Chakra is massage therapy, focusing on the lower part of your pet's body. Massaging the hips, legs, and lower back helps stimulate the energy flow through the Root Chakra, releasing tension and promoting relaxation. You can use gentle circular motions with your hands, applying light pressure to areas where your pet may hold tension. Not only does this relax the muscles, but it also encourages the release of blocked energy in the Root Chakra.

Incorporating essential oils known for their grounding properties can also be beneficial. Oils like vetiver, cedarwood, and patchouli are excellent for balancing the Root Chakra, as their earthy aromas help anchor and stabilize energy. These oils can be diffused in your pet's environment or diluted and applied topically to areas like the lower back or paws. When using essential oils on pets, it's important to dilute them properly and ensure they are safe for the species and size of your animal.

Always consult a holistic veterinarian if you're unsure about the use of essential oils for your pet.

Crystals also play a significant role in Root Chakra balancing. Stones such as red jasper, hematite, and smoky quartz are known for their grounding properties and can be placed around your pet's resting area or attached to their collar. Red jasper helps provide emotional stability and courage, making it an excellent choice for pets that are easily frightened or anxious. Hematite is a protective stone that absorbs negative energy, making it ideal for pets that are exposed to stressful environments or who react strongly to external stimuli. Smoky quartz is a gentle grounding stone that calms anxiety and helps pets feel more connected to their surroundings.

To integrate crystal healing into your pet's routine, you can create a crystal grid around their bed or favorite resting area. Place grounding stones at the four corners of their space, setting an intention for stability and security. You can also carry a grounding stone with you during walks or outings to help your pet feel more anchored while away from home.

Another technique to balance the Root Chakra is through color therapy. Since the Root Chakra resonates with the color red, incorporating this color into your pet's environment can help stimulate and balance this energy center. You can use red bedding, blankets, or toys, or even dress your pet in a red bandana or collar. While color therapy alone may not fully restore balance to the Root Chakra, it serves as a gentle complement to other holistic practices, reinforcing the energy of stability and grounding.

Sound therapy is another effective tool for Root Chakra healing. Low-frequency sounds, such as the beat of a drum or the hum of Tibetan singing bowls, resonate deeply with the Root Chakra and can help restore its balance. Playing grounding music or rhythmic drumming during your pet's relaxation time creates a calming atmosphere that supports the flow of energy through the Root Chakra. You can also use your own voice by chanting the sound "Lam," which is associated with the Root Chakra.

Chanting or playing the "Lam" sound near your pet helps to vibrate and open this energy center, promoting feelings of safety and groundedness.

If your pet struggles with deep-seated fear or insecurity, you can incorporate Reiki into their healing process. Reiki, a form of energy healing, can help clear energetic blockages in the Root Chakra and promote a sense of inner peace. During a Reiki session, the practitioner channels healing energy to the pet, focusing specifically on the Root Chakra area at the base of the spine. Reiki helps restore balance by soothing the nervous system and reestablishing a sense of stability. Even if you are not a trained Reiki practitioner, you can use your intention to send loving, grounding energy to your pet during meditation or quiet moments together.

For pets that exhibit insecurity or clinginess, creating a consistent routine is crucial for balancing the Root Chakra. Pets thrive on routine because it provides a sense of predictability and security, which is essential for Root Chakra health. By establishing regular feeding times, exercise routines, and designated rest periods, you create an environment that feels safe and stable for your pet. This routine allows them to know what to expect each day, reducing anxiety and helping them feel more grounded.

Lastly, diet plays an important role in Root Chakra balance. Foods that are rich in nutrients and align with the earth element help strengthen the Root Chakra's energy. For dogs and cats, incorporating natural, whole foods such as root vegetables (like carrots and sweet potatoes), lean proteins, and healthy fats supports their physical health and grounding energy. Avoid processed foods, as these can contribute to imbalances in the body and disrupt the flow of energy.

By addressing the Root Chakra's balance through these holistic methods, you help your pet establish a strong foundation of security and stability. A balanced Root Chakra allows your pet to feel confident in their environment, free from the fear and anxiety that can disrupt their well-being. In the next chapter, we will explore advanced techniques for unblocking and energizing the Root Chakra, providing deeper insights into how to strengthen this vital energy center.

In the previous chapter, we explored the foundational practices for balancing the Root Chakra, focusing on grounding techniques, crystals, massage, and environmental adjustments. Now, we delve into advanced methods for unblocking and energizing the Root Chakra in pets. These techniques are designed to work at a deeper energetic level, addressing chronic imbalances or situations where the pet's sense of security and stability has been severely disrupted. By strengthening the Root Chakra, you can help your pet regain confidence, alleviate fear, and improve their overall emotional and physical well-being.

One of the most effective ways to work with the Root Chakra on a deeper level is through focused energy work. This can include practices like Reiki, therapeutic touch, or simply using your intention to channel energy toward the Root Chakra. In this practice, your primary goal is to unblock any stagnant energy that might be preventing the Root Chakra from functioning properly and to energize the chakra to restore its balance. By focusing on the base of the spine, you can directly address the area where feelings of insecurity, fear, or instability reside.

To begin, find a quiet space where your pet feels comfortable and safe. You may wish to prepare the space by playing soft, grounding music or lighting a candle to set a calm atmosphere. Sit with your pet, either placing your hands gently at the base of their spine (if your pet is comfortable with touch) or hovering your hands just above the area. Close your eyes, take a few deep breaths, and set your intention to channel grounding and stabilizing energy into your pet's Root Chakra.

As you breathe, visualize a warm, red light glowing at the base of your pet's spine. This red light represents the energy of the Root Chakra, and your goal is to make this light brighter and more vibrant. Imagine the red light expanding outward with each breath, filling your pet's body with a sense of stability and security. You can imagine the energy flowing downward from the base of the spine, connecting your pet to the earth below. Visualize any blockages dissolving as the red light becomes stronger and more stable.

If your pet has experienced trauma or long-term insecurity, you may encounter moments where the energy feels "stuck" or resistant to flow. In these cases, it's important to be patient and continue breathing deeply, allowing the energy to move at its own pace. You can gently encourage the flow of energy by speaking softly to your pet, reassuring them with calming words or mantras. The sound of your voice combined with your focused intention helps release blockages and restore balance.

Another advanced technique for energizing the Root Chakra is the use of vibrational sound therapy, specifically with low-frequency sounds or drumming. The Root Chakra resonates with low, deep sounds that mimic the heartbeat of the earth, helping pets feel more grounded and connected. Playing low-frequency tones, Tibetan singing bowls, or even soft drumming can have a profound effect on your pet's Root Chakra, helping to unblock energy and promote a deep sense of calm.

Drumming is especially effective for pets that are prone to anxiety or fear, as the rhythmic beat mimics the natural rhythms of the body, creating a sense of safety and security. You don't need to be an expert drummer to use this technique—simply tapping a drum or even using your hands to create a soft, steady beat can be enough to initiate the grounding process. As you drum, focus your intention on connecting your pet's energy to the earth, allowing the sound to reverberate through their body and calm their nervous system.

Incorporating mantras into your sound therapy can amplify its effects. The mantra "Lam," associated with the Root Chakra, can be chanted softly while working with your pet. You can either chant the mantra aloud or play recordings of the sound during your energy sessions. The vibrations of "Lam" help activate the Root Chakra, promoting balance and releasing energetic blockages. As you chant or play the sound, visualize the sound waves gently flowing through your pet's body, harmonizing their energy and restoring stability.

In addition to sound therapy, light therapy can be a powerful tool for unblocking the Root Chakra. Red light therapy or chromotherapy uses the energy of color to stimulate specific chakras, and the color red is directly linked to the Root Chakra. You can use red light bulbs, lamps, or chromotherapy devices to expose your pet to healing red light. Simply placing a red light near their bed or using it during meditation or massage sessions can help energize the Root Chakra, especially when combined with other grounding techniques.

For pets that are more sensitive to light, you can introduce visualization techniques that use color. As you sit with your pet, guide your own mind to visualize a strong red light surrounding their Root Chakra, and imagine that this light is cleansing and strengthening the energy center. Visualization, combined with your focused intention, can have a powerful impact on your pet's energy, even if you are not using physical light sources.

Grounding exercises are another advanced method to strengthen the Root Chakra. Since the Root Chakra is deeply connected to the earth, encouraging your pet to engage in activities that connect them with nature can help unblock stagnant energy and restore balance. Walking barefoot on grass, digging in the dirt, or simply lying on the ground are all ways pets instinctively ground themselves.

For dogs, this could mean more time spent outdoors in natural environments, such as parks or wooded areas where they can explore, dig, and connect with the earth. For indoor pets like cats, you can create opportunities for grounding by providing them with access to outdoor spaces (if safe), placing natural elements like stones or plants around their environment, or setting up areas where they can dig or scratch. The key is to encourage activities that allow your pet to feel physically connected to the earth, as this reinforces the balance of their Root Chakra.

To further deepen the grounding effect, you can introduce earth-based essential oils during these grounding exercises. Oils like vetiver, cedarwood, and sandalwood have deep, grounding scents that align with the Root Chakra's energy. You can diffuse these oils outdoors during walks or rub diluted oils onto your pet's paws or lower back. These scents work to anchor your pet's energy, helping them feel more secure and connected to their environment.

In cases where the Root Chakra is severely blocked, it may be necessary to use more intensive practices, such as chakra cleansing through smudging or energy clearing rituals. Smudging with herbs like sage or palo santo can help clear any negative or stagnant energy that may be affecting the Root Chakra. To smudge your pet's space, light the sage or palo santo and allow the smoke to drift around the area where your pet spends time. You can also gently wave the smoke around your pet's body, paying special attention to the area near the base of the spine.

As you smudge, set the intention to clear any energetic blockages and restore balance to the Root Chakra. Visualize the smoke carrying away any negative energy, leaving your pet's energy field clear and open. Smudging can be especially beneficial after stressful events, such as a move, visit to the vet, or any situation that may have disrupted your pet's sense of security.

Once the Root Chakra has been cleansed and unblocked, it's important to maintain its balance by reinforcing grounding practices regularly. Daily routines, mindful walks, energy sessions, and Reiki can all be incorporated into your pet's holistic care plan to keep their Root Chakra in a healthy, balanced state. Maintaining this balance allows your pet to feel more confident, relaxed, and secure in their environment, leading to overall emotional and physical well-being.

Balancing the Root Chakra is a foundational step in supporting your pet's energetic health. When this chakra is strong and open, your pet is better equipped to handle life's challenges with calm and resilience. As you continue your journey in understanding the chakra system, the next chapter will explore the

Sacral Chakra, the energy center associated with creativity, emotions, and relationships. This chakra governs your pet's emotional health and their ability to connect with others, making it a key aspect of their overall well-being.

Chapter 14
Balancing Animal Chakras

The Sacral Chakra, located just below the navel, is the energy center that governs creativity, emotions, and relationships in both humans and animals. In pets, the Sacral Chakra is particularly important because it influences their emotional well-being, their ability to form healthy bonds with other animals and humans, and their capacity for pleasure and play. When the Sacral Chakra is balanced, pets experience a harmonious emotional life, express their feelings healthily, and enjoy playful and affectionate interactions. However, when this chakra is blocked or imbalanced, pets may exhibit emotional disturbances such as anxiety, depression, or aggression, as well as physical symptoms related to reproductive health or urinary issues.

The Sacral Chakra is associated with the color orange and the element of water. This connection to water reflects the fluidity of emotions and the need for emotional balance. Pets with a balanced Sacral Chakra tend to have a healthy emotional expression, enjoy playtime, and are affectionate without being overly dependent. On the other hand, pets with an imbalanced Sacral Chakra may struggle with emotional regulation, displaying either excessive clinginess or complete detachment. These imbalances can lead to mood swings, fear of abandonment, or even destructive behaviors.

One of the most common signs of a blocked Sacral Chakra is emotional instability. Pets may become excessively needy or demanding of attention, seeking constant validation from their owners. They may follow their owner from room to room, whine when left alone, or exhibit behaviors that indicate they are uncomfortable with separation. In other cases, an imbalanced Sacral Chakra can lead to emotional withdrawal, where the pet seems disinterested in interaction, play, or affection. They may spend more time alone, show less enthusiasm for activities they once enjoyed, or seem emotionally distant.

Another sign of Sacral Chakra imbalance is fear of intimacy or rejection. Pets with this imbalance may have difficulty forming trusting relationships with other animals or humans. They may be shy, fearful, or aggressive in situations that require emotional closeness, such as being petted, hugged, or groomed. This fear of emotional vulnerability can also manifest as territorial behavior, where the pet feels threatened by new people or animals entering their space.

The Sacral Chakra also influences a pet's creative and playful expression. When this chakra is in balance, pets are more likely to engage in playful behaviors, explore their environment with curiosity, and express themselves through movement, whether that's running, playing with toys, or interacting with other animals. A blocked Sacral Chakra can result in a pet becoming lethargic or disinterested in play, as if they've lost their sense of joy or spontaneity.

One effective way to begin balancing the Sacral Chakra is through water therapy. Since the Sacral Chakra is connected to the element of water, encouraging your pet to interact with water can help restore balance. For dogs, this might mean taking them swimming in a safe body of water or giving them time to splash in a shallow pool. For cats, who are typically less fond of water, simply placing bowls of water around the home or using a small water fountain can create a calming, emotionally balancing environment.

Bathing your pet in saltwater or using flower essences in their bathwater can further enhance the healing effect. Saltwater has natural cleansing properties that help clear negative energy and emotional blockages, while flower essences like Bach's Crab Apple or Star of Bethlehem can promote emotional release and healing. These remedies are particularly useful for pets that have experienced emotional trauma or loss, helping them process and release those emotions in a gentle way.

Massage therapy focused on the area of the lower abdomen and hips can also help release blocked energy in the Sacral Chakra. Using gentle, circular motions with your fingertips, you can massage this area to promote relaxation and stimulate energy flow. For pets that are sensitive to touch, you can start with light strokes and gradually increase the pressure as they become more comfortable. Massage not only helps release tension in the muscles but also allows for the energetic release of emotional blockages held in the Sacral Chakra.

In addition to massage, you can use essential oils that resonate with the Sacral Chakra's energy. Oils such as sweet orange, ylang-ylang, and sandalwood are known for their ability to balance emotions, enhance creativity, and promote emotional healing. These oils can be diffused in your pet's environment or diluted with a carrier oil and applied topically to the lower abdomen or hips. Sweet orange oil, in particular, is excellent for uplifting the mood and encouraging playfulness, while ylang-ylang helps to calm anxiety and promote emotional security.

Crystal therapy is another powerful tool for balancing the Sacral Chakra. Crystals such as carnelian, orange calcite, and moonstone are associated with this chakra and can be used to restore emotional balance. Carnelian is known for its energizing and stabilizing properties, making it ideal for pets that lack enthusiasm or seem emotionally stagnant. Orange calcite helps dissolve negative emotions and stimulates creativity, while moonstone encourages emotional healing and balance, particularly for pets that have experienced trauma or loss.

To use crystals, you can place them in your pet's resting area or attach them to their collar. If your pet enjoys being touched, you can gently place a crystal on their lower abdomen while they are lying down and allow the crystal's energy to interact with their chakra. Alternatively, creating a crystal grid in the room where your pet spends the most time can enhance the overall energy of the space, promoting emotional harmony and balance.

For pets that have a particularly strong fear of intimacy or abandonment, emotional bonding exercises can help heal the Sacral Chakra. Spend time sitting quietly with your pet, offering physical closeness and gentle reassurance without forcing interaction. Allow your pet to approach you on their own terms, giving them the space to explore intimacy at their own pace. These quiet bonding moments help build trust and encourage emotional openness, gradually easing the fear of rejection or closeness.

Music therapy that uses flowing, soothing sounds can also support the Sacral Chakra. Music with soft, rhythmic patterns or the sounds of flowing water can help calm an emotionally imbalanced pet and stimulate the fluid energy of the Sacral Chakra. You can play this type of music during relaxation periods, massage sessions, or while your pet is resting, allowing the sounds to gently influence their emotional state.

When working with the Sacral Chakra, it's important to focus on encouraging emotional expression in your pet. This could involve increasing their opportunities for play, engaging them in new activities, or simply allowing them to express their emotions through physical interaction. For pets that are emotionally withdrawn, introducing new toys, engaging in games, or spending more quality time together can help reignite their playful and creative energy.

For pets that exhibit signs of emotional trauma or have difficulty trusting others, Reiki can be particularly effective in healing the Sacral Chakra. During a Reiki session, the practitioner channels healing energy into the pet's body, focusing specifically on the area around the lower abdomen where the Sacral Chakra is located. Reiki helps to clear emotional blockages and restore the pet's ability to experience joy, connection, and emotional security.

Even if you are not a trained Reiki practitioner, you can offer your pet energy healing by simply sitting with them and setting an intention to send love and healing energy to their Sacral Chakra. Visualize a warm, orange light glowing around your pet's abdomen, expanding outward with each breath. Imagine this light filling your pet's body with emotional balance and healing energy, allowing them to release any fear, sadness, or emotional pain they may be holding.

In some cases, an imbalanced Sacral Chakra can lead to reproductive or urinary issues in pets. If you notice physical symptoms such as frequent urination, urinary infections, or problems related to reproduction, it's important to consult with a veterinarian to rule out any medical conditions. However, incorporating Sacral Chakra balancing techniques can provide additional emotional and energetic support, helping your pet recover more fully by addressing the underlying emotional imbalances that may be contributing to their physical symptoms.

Balancing the Sacral Chakra is crucial for helping your pet achieve emotional harmony, build healthy relationships, and experience joy and creativity in their daily life. By using a combination of water therapy, massage, essential oils, crystals, and energy work, you can restore balance to this vital energy center, allowing your pet to feel secure, emotionally expressive, and connected. In the next chapter, we will explore more advanced techniques for unblocking and energizing the Sacral Chakra, with a focus on healing emotional trauma and restoring emotional equilibrium in pets.

When a pet has endured emotional trauma, whether from abuse, abandonment, or significant life changes, the Sacral Chakra can become blocked, preventing the free flow of emotional energy. This blockage can lead to a disconnection from emotional expression, fear of intimacy, or difficulty forming trusting relationships. Pets may appear withdrawn, anxious, or reactive when faced with affection or emotional closeness. Advanced healing techniques for the Sacral Chakra aim to restore this emotional balance, allowing your pet to feel safe and connected again.

Healing trauma often begins with creating an emotionally safe environment. The Sacral Chakra is deeply influenced by the pet's surroundings, so it's essential to ensure that their space promotes feelings of security and calm. You can do this by incorporating elements that resonate with the Sacral Chakra, such as soft fabrics, calming scents, and warm lighting. Orange, the color associated with the Sacral Chakra, can be introduced into your pet's environment through bedding, blankets, or toys. This color promotes emotional healing and helps activate the flow of energy in the Sacral Chakra.

In addition to color therapy, aromatherapy can provide emotional support for pets recovering from trauma or dealing with emotional imbalances. Essential oils like bergamot, rose, and geranium are particularly beneficial for restoring emotional harmony and promoting feelings of comfort and safety. These oils can be diffused in your pet's space or diluted and applied to their lower abdomen, where the Sacral Chakra is located. Bergamot is known for its ability to lift the spirit and alleviate depression, while rose oil opens the heart to love and healing, and geranium helps balance emotions and calm anxiety.

For pets that have experienced deep emotional trauma, the use of flower essences can offer additional support. Star of Bethlehem is a powerful remedy for pets that have experienced shock or trauma, helping to soothe emotional wounds and promote recovery. Walnut can be used to help pets adjust to significant changes in their environment, such as a move, the loss of a companion, or the introduction of new animals. Honeysuckle is beneficial for pets that seem stuck in the past, particularly those that have difficulty moving forward after a traumatic event.

When using flower essences for trauma healing, it's important to administer them consistently over time. These essences work gently, gradually shifting the pet's emotional state by clearing blockages and restoring balance. You can add a few drops of the essence to your pet's water or food, or apply them topically to areas like the paws, nose, or directly over the Sacral Chakra. Regular use of these essences helps pets process and release emotional pain, allowing the Sacral Chakra to open and function properly.

In addition to flower essences, Reiki and other forms of energy healing can be highly effective for unblocking the Sacral Chakra and promoting emotional healing. During a Reiki session, the practitioner channels healing energy into the pet's body, focusing on the lower abdomen where the Sacral Chakra resides. Reiki helps to clear energetic blockages, release trapped emotions, and restore the pet's natural emotional flow. If you're not a trained Reiki practitioner, you can still offer energy healing to your pet by sitting quietly with them, placing your hands gently on their lower abdomen, and setting the intention to send healing energy to the Sacral Chakra.

While offering energy healing, you can visualize an orange light surrounding your pet's lower abdomen. This light represents the energy of the Sacral Chakra and helps dissolve any blockages that may be preventing the chakra from functioning properly. As you focus on this light, imagine it growing stronger and brighter, filling your pet's body with warmth, love, and emotional security. This visualization, combined with your intention, helps activate the Sacral Chakra and promotes healing.

For pets that are particularly sensitive or resistant to physical touch, sound therapy is another powerful tool for balancing the Sacral Chakra. The vibration of sound resonates deeply with this energy center, helping to clear blockages and restore balance. Instruments such as Tibetan singing bowls, chimes, or drums can be used to create healing vibrations that penetrate the pet's energy field and stimulate the Sacral Chakra. Playing soft, rhythmic music or sounds of flowing water can have a calming effect on your pet and encourage emotional release.

You can also chant the sound associated with the Sacral Chakra—"Vam"—during energy healing sessions or play recordings of this sound. The vibrations of the mantra "Vam" resonate with the Sacral Chakra and help to activate and balance its energy. Chanting or playing this sound near your pet creates a soothing, healing atmosphere that promotes emotional security and opens the pathway for emotional healing.

Crystal therapy continues to be an essential component of Sacral Chakra balancing. In addition to carnelian and orange calcite, which were introduced in the previous chapter, sunstone is another excellent crystal for healing the Sacral Chakra. Sunstone helps dispel fear and self-doubt, replacing these negative emotions with warmth, joy, and confidence. For pets that have lost their sense of joy or playfulness, sunstone can reignite their inner spark, encouraging them to express themselves more freely and with emotional openness.

To work with crystals, you can place them in your pet's environment or gently lay them on their lower abdomen while they rest. If your pet prefers not to be touched, simply keeping the crystals near them can have a beneficial effect on their energy field. You can also create a crystal grid around their bed or resting area, setting the intention for emotional healing and balance. This creates a space where the energy of the Sacral Chakra is constantly being supported and nurtured.

For pets that have experienced emotional trauma related to relationships, whether with other animals or humans, emotional bonding exercises are crucial for restoring trust and connection. These exercises help rebuild the emotional bond between you and your pet, fostering a sense of safety and emotional security. Begin by sitting quietly with your pet, offering them your undivided attention and allowing them to approach you at their own pace. Gently stroke their fur, speak softly, and provide reassurance without forcing interaction. These moments of quiet bonding help your pet feel safe and loved, allowing them to reconnect emotionally.

Play therapy is another excellent way to activate the Sacral Chakra and restore emotional balance. Encouraging your pet to engage in playful activities helps release pent-up emotions, especially for pets that have become withdrawn or emotionally stagnant. Play therapy can include anything from introducing new toys to engaging in physical games like fetch, tug-of-war, or interactive play with other animals. The key is to encourage your pet to express themselves creatively and joyfully, helping them reconnect with their innate sense of play.

For pets that are hesitant to engage in play, start with gentle encouragement, offering toys that stimulate curiosity or activities that align with their natural instincts. For example, cats may enjoy chasing feather toys or pouncing on objects, while dogs may prefer games that involve running, jumping, or retrieving. As your pet begins to engage more fully in play, their Sacral Chakra becomes more active, promoting emotional healing and a renewed sense of joy.

In some cases, pets with a blocked Sacral Chakra may exhibit reproductive or urinary issues, such as frequent urinary infections, incontinence, or hormonal imbalances. While it's important to consult a veterinarian for any medical concerns, incorporating Sacral Chakra balancing techniques can support the healing process. Acupressure or massage therapy targeting the lower abdomen can help alleviate tension in this area and promote the free flow of energy, which in turn supports the healing of physical symptoms related to the Sacral Chakra.

Finally, creating a consistent emotional routine can help maintain balance in your pet's Sacral Chakra. Pets thrive on routine, and providing regular times for bonding, play, and relaxation helps them feel emotionally secure. This routine might include daily walks, playtime, quiet time for cuddling, and moments of mindfulness where you simply sit with your pet and offer emotional support. By reinforcing this routine, you help your pet develop a sense of emotional predictability, which is essential for maintaining a balanced Sacral Chakra.

In summary, healing the Sacral Chakra on a deeper level requires a combination of advanced energy work, emotional bonding, and practices that support both emotional and physical well-being. By using techniques such as sound therapy, Reiki, aromatherapy, and play therapy, you can help your pet release emotional trauma, restore their sense of joy, and form healthy, trusting relationships. In the next chapter, we will shift our focus to the Solar Plexus Chakra, the energy center responsible for self-esteem, personal power, and emotional control, which plays a critical role in your pet's confidence and behavior.

Chapter 15
Focus on the Solar Plexus Chakra

The Solar Plexus Chakra, located just above the navel, governs an animal's sense of self-confidence, personal power, and emotional control. This chakra is closely associated with your pet's identity and autonomy, influencing how they interact with others, handle stress, and assert their boundaries. A balanced Solar Plexus Chakra allows pets to exhibit self-assurance, emotional stability, and a healthy sense of independence. However, when the Solar Plexus Chakra is blocked or imbalanced, pets may show signs of insecurity, anxiety, aggression, or timidity, often reflecting underlying issues related to self-esteem and emotional control.

The Solar Plexus Chakra is associated with the color yellow and the element of fire. This connection to fire symbolizes strength, determination, and energy, all of which are critical for your pet's ability to navigate their environment with confidence and purpose. When balanced, pets have a strong sense of who they are and what they need, expressing their desires in a calm and assertive manner. When imbalanced, however, they may exhibit behaviors that indicate insecurity, fear of authority, or overcompensation in the form of dominance or aggression.

One of the most common signs of an imbalanced Solar Plexus Chakra is insecurity or low self-esteem. Pets with a blocked Solar Plexus Chakra may shy away from challenges, avoid new situations, or become overly submissive in the presence of other animals or humans. They may cower, retreat, or display overly cautious behaviors, showing a lack of confidence in their surroundings or themselves. These pets often need constant reassurance and may exhibit clinginess or reluctance to explore new environments.

In contrast, an overactive Solar Plexus Chakra can manifest as dominance or aggressive behavior, where the pet feels the need to exert control over others to maintain a sense of power. This can lead to territorial disputes with other animals, defiance toward authority, or excessive barking and protective behavior. Pets with an overactive Solar Plexus Chakra may appear confident on the surface, but this confidence is often a mask for underlying insecurity or fear of losing control.

The key to balancing the Solar Plexus Chakra is to help your pet develop a healthy sense of self-esteem and emotional control. One of the most effective ways to begin this process is through training and positive reinforcement. Structured training exercises help pets understand their place in the family hierarchy and develop a sense of confidence in their abilities. Training that focuses on positive reinforcement—rewarding good behavior with treats, praise, or affection—encourages your pet to act confidently and assertively without becoming dominant or aggressive.

When training your pet, it's important to establish clear boundaries and expectations, as this helps them feel secure in their role within the family. Pets with a balanced Solar Plexus Chakra thrive in environments where they understand what is expected of them and where they are rewarded for good behavior. This structure not only builds their self-esteem but also helps them learn emotional control, preventing the outbursts of aggression or fear that can arise from a blocked or overactive Solar Plexus Chakra.

In addition to training, exercise plays a crucial role in balancing the Solar Plexus Chakra. Since this chakra is connected to the element of fire, physical activity helps burn off excess energy and promote a sense of calm control. Regular exercise, such as running, walking, or playing fetch, allows your pet to release pent-up energy in a positive way, reducing the likelihood of aggressive or anxious behavior. For high-energy pets, incorporating games that challenge their mind and body—like agility courses or puzzle toys—can further enhance their sense of accomplishment and confidence.

Another method for balancing the Solar Plexus Chakra is through massage therapy, focusing on the upper abdomen, where this chakra is located. Gentle massage in this area helps release tension and stimulate energy flow, promoting a sense of relaxation and emotional stability. You can use slow, circular motions with your fingertips, starting from the center of the pet's abdomen and moving outward. If your pet enjoys physical touch, this can be a deeply calming experience that helps restore balance to the Solar Plexus Chakra.

Essential oils are also powerful tools for healing the Solar Plexus Chakra. Oils such as ginger, lemon, and peppermint are known for their ability to energize and balance this chakra. These oils can be diffused in your pet's environment to create a soothing atmosphere or diluted with a carrier oil and applied topically to the upper abdomen. Ginger promotes courage and self-assurance, helping pets overcome fear or insecurity, while lemon uplifts the mood and enhances mental clarity. Peppermint is invigorating and helps stimulate the flow of energy, making it ideal for pets that are lethargic or lack motivation.

Crystal therapy is another effective way to balance the Solar Plexus Chakra. Crystals such as citrine, yellow jasper, and tiger's eye resonate with this chakra's energy and can be used to promote confidence, emotional control, and a sense of personal power. Citrine is known as the stone of abundance and self-worth, making it an excellent choice for pets that need help developing their confidence and assertiveness. Yellow jasper is grounding and protective, helping pets feel secure in their surroundings, while tiger's eye enhances focus and emotional stability, preventing outbursts of aggression or fear.

To use crystals for healing the Solar Plexus Chakra, you can place them in your pet's resting area or attach them to their collar. If your pet is comfortable with touch, you can gently lay the crystal on their upper abdomen while they rest, allowing the stone's energy to interact with their chakra. Alternatively, creating a crystal grid around your pet's space can help amplify the healing energy and promote long-term balance.

Sunlight therapy is particularly beneficial for the Solar Plexus Chakra, as this chakra is associated with the sun's energy. Spending time outdoors in the sunlight helps to activate and energize this chakra, promoting confidence and vitality. Allow your pet to bask in the sun for short periods, making sure they are safe and comfortable. Sunlight not only helps balance the Solar Plexus Chakra but also improves mood and overall well-being.

For pets that exhibit signs of fear or insecurity, Reiki can be an effective tool for restoring balance to the Solar Plexus Chakra. During a Reiki session, the practitioner channels healing energy into the pet's body, focusing on the upper abdomen where this chakra is located. Reiki helps to clear energetic blockages, release fear, and restore a sense of emotional stability. Even if you're not a trained Reiki practitioner, you can offer energy healing to your pet by placing your hands gently on their upper abdomen and visualizing a warm, yellow light surrounding the area.

As you focus on this yellow light, imagine it growing stronger and brighter, filling your pet's body with warmth and confidence. This visualization, combined with your intention, helps activate the Solar Plexus Chakra and promotes healing. You can also use the mantra "Ram," which is associated with the Solar Plexus Chakra, to enhance the healing process. Chanting or playing recordings of this sound creates a vibration that resonates with the chakra, promoting balance and emotional control.

Incorporating structured play into your pet's routine is another way to stimulate the Solar Plexus Chakra. Games that challenge your pet's mind and body—such as hide-and-seek, fetch, or agility exercises—help build their confidence and self-esteem. These activities encourage your pet to take initiative, solve problems, and assert their independence, all of which strengthen the Solar Plexus Chakra.

For pets that struggle with aggression or dominance, it's important to focus on emotional regulation and reinforcing positive behaviors. You can use calming techniques such as breathing exercises or mindful walks to help your pet develop emotional control. During a mindful walk, take slow, deliberate steps with your pet, encouraging them to stay focused on the present moment. This practice helps calm the nervous system and reinforces a sense of emotional stability.

Diet also plays a significant role in balancing the Solar Plexus Chakra. Foods that are nourishing and energizing, such as lean proteins, whole grains, and yellow-colored fruits and vegetables (like squash or bananas), help support this chakra's energy. Avoid processed foods or treats that can cause energy imbalances and disrupt your pet's mood.

Lastly, routine is essential for maintaining balance in the Solar Plexus Chakra. Pets thrive on structure, and establishing a regular routine for feeding, exercise, and play helps them feel secure and confident. By creating consistency in your pet's daily life, you reinforce their sense of stability and emotional control, preventing the fear or insecurity that can arise from a blocked Solar Plexus Chakra.

Balancing the Solar Plexus Chakra is crucial for promoting confidence, emotional stability, and healthy boundaries in pets. By using a combination of training, exercise, massage, essential oils, crystals, and energy work, you can help your pet restore their sense of self-worth and emotional control. In the next chapter, we will explore advanced techniques for further unblocking and energizing the Solar Plexus Chakra, with a focus on building trust, assertiveness, and emotional resilience in your pet.

Building on the previous exploration of the Solar Plexus Chakra, this chapter delves into more advanced techniques to unblock and energize this vital energy center, particularly focusing on fostering trust, assertiveness, and emotional resilience in pets. As we've discussed, the Solar Plexus Chakra governs self-confidence, emotional regulation, and personal power, playing a significant role in how pets express themselves and interact with their environment. When this chakra is balanced, pets demonstrate calm assertiveness, emotional stability, and a healthy sense of independence. However, deeper blockages in the Solar Plexus Chakra may require more intensive healing to restore your pet's full emotional and physical potential.

One of the most significant areas of focus in advanced Solar Plexus Chakra healing is helping pets develop assertiveness without aggression. Many pets with a blocked or imbalanced Solar Plexus Chakra either struggle with passivity, leading to insecurity, or exhibit aggression as a form of overcompensation. In these cases, it's essential to teach pets how to assert themselves confidently and calmly, without relying on fear or dominance.

Behavioral training is a key component in this process. Advanced training techniques, such as those used in agility courses, obedience competitions, or scent work, provide mental and physical challenges that build self-confidence and assertiveness in a controlled manner. These activities encourage pets to take initiative, make decisions, and solve problems, all while learning to regulate their emotions and responses. As they successfully navigate these challenges, their Solar Plexus Chakra becomes more balanced, reinforcing their sense of personal power.

For pets that lean toward dominance or aggression, it's crucial to balance assertiveness training with emotional regulation techniques. This might involve teaching your pet to pause before reacting to a stimulus or using commands to redirect their attention during moments of heightened emotion. For example, if your dog exhibits territorial behavior when someone approaches your home, you can train them to respond to a command like "sit" or "stay," helping them learn to manage their emotions and assert themselves calmly rather than aggressively.

In addition to training, incorporating energy healing practices such as Reiki or acupressure can help unblock deep energetic blockages in the Solar Plexus Chakra. Reiki, in particular, is useful for pets that have unresolved emotional trauma, anxiety, or fear that impacts their self-confidence. During a Reiki session, the practitioner channels healing energy to the

Solar Plexus Chakra, helping to release trapped emotions and restore balance. You can also practice hands-on healing with your pet by placing your hands on their upper abdomen and visualizing a bright yellow light expanding from the chakra, filling their body with warmth, confidence, and calm energy.

Acupressure is another effective tool for promoting the flow of energy through the Solar Plexus Chakra. This ancient practice involves applying gentle pressure to specific points on the body that correspond to the chakra system. For the Solar Plexus Chakra, points located around the upper abdomen or the middle of the back can help release tension and restore the natural flow of energy. You can either work with a trained practitioner or learn basic acupressure techniques that allow you to support your pet's energetic health at home.

For pets that exhibit anxiety or insecurity, aromatherapy can provide emotional support and help open the Solar Plexus Chakra. Essential oils like bergamot, ginger, and lemongrass are excellent choices for balancing this chakra, as they promote courage, mental clarity, and self-assurance. You can diffuse these oils in your pet's environment to create a calming atmosphere or dilute them with a carrier oil and apply them topically to your pet's upper abdomen. The uplifting scents of these oils help dispel fear and insecurity, allowing your pet to approach challenges with a sense of confidence and ease.

In addition to aromatherapy, sound therapy can be highly beneficial in balancing the Solar Plexus Chakra, particularly for pets that are sensitive to external stimuli. The Solar Plexus Chakra resonates with the sound "Ram," and chanting or playing this sound during meditation or energy healing sessions helps activate and clear the chakra. Instruments such as Tibetan bowls or drums that produce low, resonant tones can also help restore balance by creating vibrations that penetrate deeply into the pet's energy field, encouraging emotional release and stability.

For pets that have experienced trauma related to authority figures or feel disempowered, bonding and trust-building exercises are essential. These exercises help your pet develop a sense of emotional security and trust, which is necessary for a balanced Solar Plexus Chakra. Start by creating opportunities for positive, non-threatening interactions that allow your pet to build confidence in a safe and controlled environment. This might involve quiet, one-on-one time where you offer gentle reassurance and support, encouraging your pet to approach and interact at their own pace.

Eye contact exercises are particularly useful for building trust and emotional connection, especially with pets that are shy or anxious. By maintaining soft, non-threatening eye contact while offering praise or treats, you help your pet associate positive emotions with direct interaction, reinforcing their sense of trust and security. Over time, these exercises help strengthen the Solar Plexus Chakra by encouraging your pet to feel more empowered and in control of their emotional responses.

Play therapy is another excellent way to stimulate the Solar Plexus Chakra and promote emotional healing. Games that encourage exploration and problem-solving—such as hide-and-seek, puzzle toys, or scent games—help pets engage their mental and physical faculties while building self-confidence. For dogs, agility training or obstacle courses can provide a structured way to channel their energy and develop a sense of accomplishment. For cats, interactive toys that mimic hunting behavior or encourage exploration can be equally effective in boosting their sense of personal power and assertiveness.

For pets that exhibit signs of overdominance or aggression, dietary adjustments can support emotional regulation and balance. Incorporating foods that resonate with the Solar Plexus Chakra's energy—such as yellow-colored fruits and vegetables, lean proteins, and whole grains—can help stabilize energy levels and promote emotional well-being. Avoid processed foods or treats that may cause spikes in energy followed by crashes, as these can exacerbate emotional imbalances. Instead, focus on providing a balanced, nutrient-rich diet that supports both physical and energetic health.

Crystal therapy continues to play an essential role in balancing the Solar Plexus Chakra. In addition to citrine, yellow jasper, and tiger's eye, amber is an excellent crystal for promoting emotional healing and balance in the Solar Plexus Chakra. Amber's warm, nurturing energy helps pets feel safe and protected, while also promoting emotional clarity and calmness. For pets that struggle with aggression, yellow calcite is another effective crystal, as it helps soothe emotional tension and encourages positive, balanced self-expression.

To use crystals in healing sessions, you can place them around your pet's resting area or gently lay them on their upper abdomen while they relax. Creating a crystal grid in your pet's space helps amplify the energy of the Solar Plexus Chakra, promoting long-term balance and emotional stability. You can also carry a small crystal with you during walks or training sessions to provide continuous support for your pet's emotional health.

Lastly, mindfulness practices such as meditation or guided visualizations can help both you and your pet achieve greater emotional balance. Sit quietly with your pet in a calm, comfortable space, and focus on your breath while visualizing a warm, golden light filling your pet's body. This light represents the energy of the Solar Plexus Chakra, and as it grows brighter, imagine it clearing away any negative emotions, fear, or insecurity. This practice not only helps balance your pet's chakra but also strengthens the bond between you, promoting a sense of shared emotional calmness and resilience.

In conclusion, balancing the Solar Plexus Chakra requires a combination of advanced energy work, behavioral training, emotional bonding, and physical care. By using techniques such as Reiki, acupressure, crystal therapy, and structured play, you can help your pet restore their sense of personal power, emotional stability, and confidence. These practices promote a deeper connection between you and your pet, helping them navigate the world with calm assertiveness and emotional resilience. In the next chapter, we will explore the Heart Chakra, which governs love, compassion, and emotional connection, and plays a crucial role in your pet's ability to form deep, loving bonds with others.

Chapter 16
Focus on the Heart Chakra

The Heart Chakra is the center of love, compassion, and emotional connection in both humans and animals. Located in the chest, this chakra governs the ability to give and receive love, form deep bonds, and maintain emotional balance. In pets, a balanced Heart Chakra allows for healthy relationships with both humans and other animals, fostering trust, affection, and empathy. When this chakra is in balance, pets are loving, social, and emotionally secure. However, an imbalanced or blocked Heart Chakra can lead to behavioral issues such as apathy, fear of relationships, or excessive clinginess, as pets struggle to either give or receive love.

The Heart Chakra is associated with the color green and the element of air, symbolizing emotional openness, harmony, and connection. A balanced Heart Chakra enables pets to express love freely and confidently, engaging in positive interactions with those around them. However, when the chakra is blocked, pets may become withdrawn, fearful of relationships, or overly dependent, seeking constant validation and attention from their owners. On the other hand, an overactive Heart Chakra can manifest as excessive clinginess, where the pet may struggle with separation anxiety or an inability to tolerate any distance from their owner.

Pets with a blocked Heart Chakra may show signs of emotional detachment or aloofness. They might avoid physical affection, such as petting or cuddling, and may seem uninterested in social interactions, whether with humans or other animals. These pets often appear indifferent, spending more time alone and engaging less in playful or affectionate behaviors. In extreme cases, a blocked Heart Chakra can lead to depression in pets, where they lose interest in activities they once enjoyed and become emotionally stagnant.

In contrast, pets with an overactive Heart Chakra may exhibit separation anxiety or clinginess, constantly seeking their owner's attention and showing signs of distress when left alone. These pets may follow their owner from room to room, whine when separated, or display destructive behavior, such as chewing furniture or excessive barking, when they are unable to maintain close physical contact. This overdependence can be emotionally draining for both the pet and the owner, as the pet struggles to regulate their emotions without constant reassurance.

To balance the Heart Chakra, it is essential to promote a healthy flow of love and emotional energy, allowing pets to feel secure in their relationships while also encouraging emotional independence. One of the most effective ways to begin balancing this chakra is through emotional bonding exercises that strengthen the relationship between pet and owner while fostering healthy boundaries. These exercises involve spending quality time with your pet, offering physical affection and reassurance, but also gradually encouraging independence by allowing the pet to explore or engage in activities on their own.

For pets that are emotionally withdrawn or avoidant, gentle touch therapy can help open the Heart Chakra and restore emotional balance. Begin by offering light, soothing strokes along your pet's chest, where the Heart Chakra is located. Use slow, deliberate movements to create a calming effect, encouraging your pet to relax and become more receptive to physical affection. Over time, this practice helps break down emotional barriers, allowing your pet to feel safe in giving and receiving love.

Crystals are a powerful tool for balancing the Heart Chakra. Stones such as rose quartz, green aventurine, and jade resonate with the energy of this chakra and can be used to promote emotional healing and openness. Rose quartz is known as the stone of unconditional love and is particularly effective for pets that have experienced emotional trauma or abandonment, helping to heal their emotional wounds and restore their ability to trust. Green aventurine promotes emotional balance and harmony, while jade encourages compassion and emotional well-being.

To use crystals in Heart Chakra healing, you can place them in your pet's resting area or gently lay them on their chest while they relax. If your pet is comfortable with touch, you can also hold a crystal in your hand while gently massaging the chest area. The energy of the crystals helps to open the Heart Chakra and create a space for emotional healing. Alternatively, you can create a crystal grid around your pet's bed or favorite resting spot, setting the intention for love, healing, and emotional balance.

Aromatherapy can also play a crucial role in balancing the Heart Chakra, especially for pets that struggle with emotional detachment or anxiety. Essential oils such as lavender, rose, and bergamot are known for their ability to soothe emotional tension and promote feelings of love and security. These oils can be diffused in your pet's environment to create a calming atmosphere or diluted with a carrier oil and applied topically to the chest area, where the Heart Chakra is located. Lavender is particularly effective for calming anxiety and promoting relaxation, while rose oil encourages emotional healing and helps pets feel safe and loved.

For pets that are overly dependent or clingy, it's important to help them develop emotional resilience and independence. One effective method for promoting emotional independence is gradual desensitization, where the pet is slowly exposed to short periods of separation from their owner in a controlled and positive manner. Start by leaving your pet alone for just a few minutes at a time, gradually increasing the duration as they become more comfortable with being alone. Offer praise and rewards when they handle the separation calmly, reinforcing positive behavior and helping them build confidence in their ability to manage their emotions without constant physical contact.

In addition to desensitization, play therapy can help balance the Heart Chakra by encouraging emotional expression through playful interaction. Games that involve gentle, cooperative play—such as fetch, tug-of-war, or hide-and-seek—

allow pets to engage with their owners in a way that reinforces emotional connection without fostering dependence. Play therapy helps pets express their love and affection in a healthy, balanced way, strengthening the bond between pet and owner while promoting emotional independence.

Reiki and other forms of energy healing are particularly effective for pets with deeply blocked or overactive Heart Chakras. During a Reiki session, the practitioner channels healing energy into the pet's body, focusing on the chest area where the Heart Chakra is located. Reiki helps to clear energetic blockages, release emotional pain, and restore the pet's natural ability to give and receive love. Even if you are not a trained Reiki practitioner, you can offer energy healing to your pet by placing your hands on their chest and visualizing a soft green or pink light surrounding the area. This light represents the energy of the Heart Chakra, and as it expands, it helps to heal emotional wounds and restore balance.

Breathing exercises can also be used to promote emotional calmness and balance in the Heart Chakra. Sit quietly with your pet and focus on your breath, taking slow, deep inhalations and exhalations. As you breathe, visualize the green energy of the Heart Chakra expanding with each breath, filling your pet's chest with love, compassion, and emotional security. This practice not only helps balance your pet's energy but also creates a calming, connected experience for both of you.

For pets that have experienced emotional trauma, such as the loss of a companion or abandonment, flower essences like Star of Bethlehem and Holly can offer gentle emotional healing. Star of Bethlehem is known for its ability to soothe shock and trauma, helping pets recover from emotional wounds and open their hearts to love again. Holly is useful for pets that exhibit jealousy or fear of rejection, helping to dissolve negative emotions and promote feelings of love and acceptance.

Lastly, maintaining a balanced routine of affection, play, and quiet time helps support the emotional health of pets with Heart Chakra imbalances. Pets thrive on routine, and creating a predictable schedule for bonding activities—such as daily walks, play sessions, and quiet cuddle time—helps them feel emotionally secure. By providing consistent emotional support, you create an environment where your pet feels safe to express love while also fostering independence.

Balancing the Heart Chakra is essential for promoting emotional connection, love, and compassion in pets. By using a combination of emotional bonding, crystal therapy, aromatherapy, play therapy, and energy healing, you can help your pet restore balance to this chakra, allowing them to give and receive love in a healthy, secure way. In the next chapter, we will explore more advanced techniques for deepening the healing of the Heart Chakra, with a focus on emotional trauma and promoting long-term emotional well-being in your pet.

Deepening the healing of the Heart Chakra requires an understanding of the intricate emotional world of animals. Pets, like humans, experience a wide range of emotions, and their capacity for love, connection, and emotional healing is profound. However, when pets have been through emotional trauma, such as the loss of a companion, abandonment, or mistreatment, their Heart Chakra can become severely blocked. In this chapter, we explore advanced techniques to unblock, open, and nurture the Heart Chakra, promoting deep emotional healing and long-term emotional well-being.

One of the key aspects of healing a deeply blocked Heart Chakra is addressing the emotional wounds that caused the blockage. Pets that have experienced trauma may exhibit signs of emotional withdrawal, fear of relationships, or difficulty trusting others. These emotional wounds can manifest as physical tension in the chest area, avoidance of eye contact, or reluctance to engage in social or affectionate behaviors. To help heal these wounds, it's essential to approach the healing process with patience, empathy, and consistency, gradually building trust and emotional security.

Crystals continue to play a crucial role in the deep healing of the Heart Chakra. In addition to rose quartz and green aventurine, which promote love and emotional balance, rhodochrosite is particularly effective for healing emotional trauma. This crystal has a nurturing energy that helps dissolve emotional pain and encourages the pet to open their heart to love once more. Malachite, another powerful stone, works by absorbing negative emotions and releasing blocked energy, making it ideal for pets that have experienced deep emotional distress.

To work with crystals for deeper Heart Chakra healing, place them on or near your pet's chest while they are resting, or create a crystal grid around their favorite relaxation spot. Visualize the healing energy of the crystals flowing into your pet's Heart Chakra, gently dissolving any emotional pain and allowing love to flow freely. Over time, this practice helps to clear emotional blockages and restore balance to the Heart Chakra.

In addition to crystal therapy, Reiki or other forms of energy healing can be used to address deeper emotional trauma. During a Reiki session, the practitioner focuses on the Heart Chakra, channeling healing energy to release trapped emotions and restore the natural flow of love and compassion. If you are not a trained Reiki practitioner, you can still offer energy healing to your pet by sitting quietly with them, placing your hands gently on their chest, and visualizing a soft green light radiating from their Heart Chakra. This green light represents healing, compassion, and love, helping to open the Heart Chakra and promote emotional healing.

For pets that are reluctant to receive physical touch, distance Reiki or simply sitting near them and sending healing energy can be equally effective. The goal is to create a space where your pet feels safe, supported, and loved, allowing them to begin the process of emotional healing at their own pace.

Emotional trauma often creates deep energetic blockages in the Heart Chakra, making it difficult for pets to trust again. For these pets, it's important to create a calm and emotionally safe environment. Start by establishing a predictable routine that includes moments of quiet bonding, such as sitting together in a calm space, offering gentle reassurance through soft words and slow, deliberate movements. Pets thrive on consistency, and knowing what to expect helps them feel more secure and open to emotional healing.

Sound therapy can also be a powerful tool for unblocking the Heart Chakra. Soft, soothing sounds such as Tibetan singing bowls or chimes resonate with the Heart Chakra, helping to release blocked energy and promote emotional balance. The sound "Yam" is specifically associated with the Heart Chakra, and chanting or playing recordings of this sound can help to activate and open the chakra. For pets that are sensitive to sound, playing gentle music or nature sounds that mimic the calming rhythm of the heart can create a peaceful atmosphere that supports emotional healing.

For pets that struggle with separation anxiety or clinginess, it's important to help them develop emotional independence while maintaining a loving connection. One effective technique is gradual desensitization, where you slowly increase the time spent apart from your pet, helping them build confidence in their ability to manage without constant physical contact. Start by leaving your pet for short intervals, gradually extending the time as they become more comfortable. Provide a safe, cozy space for your pet while you're away, and offer plenty of praise and rewards when they handle the separation calmly.

Play therapy can also be used to foster emotional resilience in pets with overactive Heart Chakras. Interactive games that engage both the body and mind—such as puzzle toys, fetch, or scent games—help pets channel their emotional energy in a positive way, promoting confidence and emotional stability. These activities allow pets to express love and excitement without becoming overly dependent on their owner's constant presence.

For pets that have experienced the loss of a companion, either human or animal, the grief can deeply affect their Heart Chakra. They may become withdrawn, lethargic, or overly attached to their remaining family members. In such cases, flower essences like Star of Bethlehem and Honeysuckle can help ease the pain of loss and promote emotional healing. Star of Bethlehem is known for its ability to soothe shock and trauma, helping pets recover from emotional wounds, while Honeysuckle helps them move forward after loss, reducing feelings of grief or nostalgia for the past.

In addition to flower essences, spending quiet time with your grieving pet can be incredibly healing. Simply sitting together in a peaceful environment, offering gentle strokes or soft words, helps your pet feel supported and loved during their healing process. Over time, this emotional support encourages the Heart Chakra to reopen, allowing your pet to process their grief and move forward with emotional balance.

Aromatherapy is another tool that can help pets with blocked Heart Chakras, especially those recovering from emotional trauma or grief. Essential oils like rose, lavender, and frankincense have powerful heart-opening properties and can be used to promote love, calmness, and emotional healing. You can diffuse these oils in your pet's environment or dilute them with a carrier oil and apply them to their chest, where the Heart Chakra is located. These calming scents help to create a peaceful atmosphere, encouraging emotional release and balance.

For pets that have difficulty forming bonds with other animals or humans, emotional bonding exercises are key to promoting connection and trust. Start by offering your pet plenty of positive reinforcement during social interactions, rewarding them with treats or praise when they engage with others in a calm and positive way. Gradually increase the duration of these interactions, allowing your pet to build confidence and trust at their own pace.

Eye contact exercises can also help strengthen the emotional bond between you and your pet, particularly for pets that struggle with emotional connection. By maintaining soft, non-threatening eye contact while offering treats or praise, you help your pet associate eye contact with positive feelings, reinforcing their emotional bond with you. This practice helps to break down emotional barriers and opens the Heart Chakra, allowing love to flow more freely between you and your pet.

Finally, creating a balanced routine of affection, play, and quiet time is essential for maintaining emotional health in pets with Heart Chakra imbalances. Pets thrive on routine, and by providing regular opportunities for bonding and emotional connection—such as daily walks, play sessions, and quiet cuddle time—you help your pet feel secure and emotionally supported. At the same time, encouraging periods of independence, where your pet can explore or engage in activities on their own, helps to prevent overdependence and fosters emotional resilience.

In summary, deepening the healing of the Heart Chakra requires a combination of energy work, emotional bonding, crystal therapy, sound therapy, and aromatherapy. By addressing the root causes of emotional trauma and promoting emotional independence, you can help your pet restore balance to their Heart Chakra, allowing them to give and receive love in a healthy, secure way. In the next chapter, we will explore the Throat Chakra, which governs communication and expression, and how balancing this chakra can improve your pet's ability to express their needs and emotions clearly and confidently.

Chapter 17
Focus on the Throat Chakra

The Throat Chakra governs communication and self-expression, making it a critical energy center for both animals and humans. Located in the throat area, this chakra influences how animals communicate their needs, desires, and emotions, whether through vocalizations, body language, or behavior. A balanced Throat Chakra allows pets to express themselves clearly and confidently, ensuring that their needs are understood and met. When this chakra is blocked or imbalanced, however, pets may struggle with communication issues, ranging from excessive vocalization to complete withdrawal, or they may display behaviors that indicate frustration or misunderstanding.

The Throat Chakra is associated with the color blue and the element of sound. A balanced Throat Chakra helps pets feel secure in expressing themselves, allowing them to vocalize their needs in a calm and controlled manner. Pets with a balanced Throat Chakra are likely to communicate their desires—such as the need for food, attention, or play—in ways that are easy for their owners to understand, whether through barking, meowing, body language, or other cues. On the other hand, an imbalanced Throat Chakra can lead to communication difficulties, either in the form of overexpression—such as constant barking or meowing—or underexpression, where the pet becomes silent, withdrawn, or unable to communicate effectively.

When the Throat Chakra is overactive, pets may vocalize excessively, often using barking, whining, or meowing to get attention or express frustration. These vocalizations may be persistent and difficult to control, as the pet struggles to regulate their communication. In some cases, pets with an overactive Throat Chakra may become overly demanding or even aggressive, using their voice to assert control or dominance in their environment. This excessive vocalization can lead to misunderstandings, as the pet's needs may not be clear or easily interpreted by their owner.

In contrast, pets with an underactive or blocked Throat Chakra may struggle to express their needs at all. These pets might become withdrawn, avoiding communication or interactions altogether. They may sit quietly, avoid eye contact, or fail to respond when called or offered attention. This withdrawal can lead to frustration on both sides, as the pet's needs go unmet due to their inability or reluctance to communicate. In some cases, a blocked Throat Chakra can lead to physical symptoms, such as issues with the throat, neck, or vocal cords, as the energy in this area becomes stagnant.

To begin balancing the Throat Chakra, it's essential to first observe your pet's communication patterns and identify any imbalances. Pets that are overly vocal may need help in learning how to communicate more calmly, while pets that are withdrawn may need encouragement to express themselves. The goal of balancing the Throat Chakra is to create an open and clear channel for communication, allowing your pet to express their needs confidently but without overwhelming themselves or those around them.

One of the most effective ways to balance the Throat Chakra is through sound therapy. Because this chakra is associated with the element of sound, using specific sounds or tones can help restore balance and promote healthy communication. The sound "Ham" is connected to the Throat Chakra, and chanting or playing recordings of this sound can help activate and clear the chakra. You can also use instruments such as Tibetan bowls, bells, or chimes that resonate with the frequencies of the Throat Chakra. These sounds create vibrations that penetrate deeply into the pet's energy field, helping to release blockages and restore the natural flow of communication.

Crystal therapy can also play a significant role in balancing the Throat Chakra. Stones such as blue lace agate, sodalite, and aquamarine resonate with the energy of this chakra and can be used to promote clear, calm communication. Blue lace agate is particularly effective for pets that are overly vocal or anxious, as it helps soothe communication and reduce excessive expression. Sodalite promotes balance and emotional control, helping pets express themselves in a more measured and calm way. Aquamarine is known for its calming properties and is especially useful for pets that are fearful or reluctant to communicate.

To use crystals for Throat Chakra healing, place them near your pet's bed or favorite resting area, or gently lay them on your pet's throat while they relax. If your pet is comfortable with touch, you can also hold a crystal in your hand and gently stroke their throat area, visualizing the crystal's energy flowing into the Throat Chakra and creating an open channel for communication. Alternatively, creating a crystal grid in your pet's environment can help amplify the healing energy and promote long-term balance in the Throat Chakra.

Massage therapy is another effective method for balancing the Throat Chakra. Gently massaging the throat area, using slow, circular motions with your fingers, helps stimulate energy flow and release tension. Be mindful to use a light touch, as the throat is a sensitive area. This type of massage not only promotes relaxation but also encourages the pet to feel more comfortable expressing themselves, both vocally and through body language.

Aromatherapy can also support the healing of the Throat Chakra, especially for pets that are anxious or reluctant to communicate. Essential oils such as chamomile, lavender, and eucalyptus are known for their calming properties and can help soothe both physical and emotional tension in the throat area. Diffusing these oils in your pet's environment creates a peaceful atmosphere that encourages open communication, while diluted applications to the throat area can help release energetic blockages. Eucalyptus in particular is beneficial for pets that have physical issues related to the throat or respiratory system, as it promotes clear breathing and energy flow in this area.

For pets that struggle with overexpression, it's important to implement techniques that help them regulate their vocalizations. Training exercises that focus on reinforcing calm behavior are particularly effective. For example, teaching your dog the "quiet" command during moments of excessive barking helps them learn to control their vocal output. Pairing the command with positive reinforcement—such as treats or praise—encourages your pet to vocalize only when necessary and to do so in a calm manner.

In addition to training, structured play can help channel excessive energy in pets that are overly vocal. Interactive games such as fetch, tug-of-war, or agility exercises help pets release pent-up energy in a positive way, reducing the likelihood of excessive vocalization caused by frustration or boredom. These activities also give pets an outlet for self-expression, allowing them to communicate through body language and play rather than through constant vocalization.

For pets that are withdrawn or struggle to express their needs, it's important to create an environment that encourages communication. Start by offering positive reinforcement whenever your pet vocalizes or uses body language to communicate. For example, when your cat meows or uses a paw to tap you for attention, reward them with affection or treats. Over time, this positive reinforcement helps build your pet's confidence in their ability to communicate and express their needs.

Eye contact exercises can also help encourage communication, particularly in pets that are shy or reluctant to engage. Maintaining soft, non-threatening eye contact while offering praise or treats helps reinforce the emotional connection between you and your pet, making them feel more comfortable expressing themselves. This practice helps open the Throat Chakra, creating a clear channel for communication through both vocalizations and body language.

Breathing exercises are particularly beneficial for pets with an overactive Throat Chakra, as they help calm the nervous system and promote emotional regulation. You can practice deep breathing exercises with your pet by sitting quietly together, focusing on slow, deep inhalations and exhalations. As you breathe, visualize a blue light expanding from your pet's throat area, helping to calm their energy and balance the Throat Chakra. This practice not only helps reduce excessive vocalization but also strengthens the bond between you and your pet, promoting a sense of calm and emotional connection.

In some cases, Reiki or other forms of energy healing can be particularly effective for pets with deeply blocked or overactive Throat Chakras. During a Reiki session, the practitioner channels healing energy into the pet's throat area, helping to release emotional blockages and restore the natural flow of communication. Even if you are not a trained Reiki practitioner, you can offer energy healing to your pet by placing your hands gently on their throat and visualizing a calming blue light surrounding the area. This blue light represents the energy of the Throat Chakra, and as it expands, it helps to clear any blockages and promote healthy, balanced communication.

Balancing the Throat Chakra is essential for promoting clear, confident communication in pets. By using techniques such as sound therapy, crystal healing, aromatherapy, and positive reinforcement, you can help your pet express their needs in a calm and controlled manner, reducing frustration and promoting emotional well-being. In the next chapter, we will explore more advanced techniques for unblocking and energizing the Throat Chakra, with a focus on enhancing your pet's ability to communicate clearly and confidently.

To further deepen the healing and balancing of the Throat Chakra, we need to explore more advanced techniques that focus on refining your pet's communication abilities and enhancing their confidence in expressing their needs. In animals, communication isn't only verbal. It's a combination of vocalizations, body language, and behavior. This chapter will dive into ways to unblock and energize the Throat Chakra, with a specific focus on improving both physical and energetic aspects of your pet's communication.

One of the most effective ways to work with the Throat Chakra is by combining energy healing with vocal and sound therapies. Because this chakra is deeply connected to sound and vibration, introducing more intentional sound-based healing practices can make a significant difference in your pet's ability to communicate. A powerful practice involves the use of mantras or toning, particularly using the sound "Ham," which is traditionally associated with the Throat Chakra. Chanting or playing this sound during meditation or healing sessions helps activate the chakra and promotes a clearer flow of communication energy. For pets that are responsive to sound, you can sit with them in a quiet space and play or chant the sound softly, visualizing their Throat Chakra opening and allowing for more fluid and healthy expression.

Another aspect of sound therapy that can be beneficial is the use of Tibetan singing bowls, tuning forks, or vocal tuning exercises that resonate with the frequencies of the Throat Chakra. Instruments that produce deep, resonant tones—especially in the key of G, which corresponds to this chakra—can create a healing environment that helps unblock stagnant energy in the throat area. Using these instruments near your pet or gently playing them in their space can have a calming and grounding effect, which helps pets that either vocalize excessively or struggle to communicate at all.

For pets that have blockages or tension in the throat and neck area, massage therapy and acupressure can also help stimulate energy flow in the Throat Chakra. Gently massaging the neck and throat, focusing on slow circular motions, helps relax physical tension while also encouraging the release of emotional or energetic blockages. Incorporating acupressure points located near the base of the skull or along the neck can further support the release of energy in this area. Always use a light touch, as these areas can be sensitive for pets.

Acupressure can be particularly effective when combined with aromatherapy. Essential oils such as chamomile, peppermint, and eucalyptus are known for their soothing properties and can help calm the throat and respiratory system, which is often linked to the Throat Chakra. You can apply a diluted blend of these oils to the throat area while performing a gentle massage or acupressure. Not only does this help physically relax the muscles around the throat, but it also supports the opening of energetic channels, allowing for more balanced expression.

For pets that are overly vocal and seem to demand constant attention through barking, meowing, or whining, it's important to create boundaries that still encourage healthy communication but reduce overexpression. Behavioral training focusing on "quiet" commands, paired with positive reinforcement, can help your pet learn to express their needs in more controlled ways. Start by teaching your pet to respond to the "quiet" command in moments of excessive vocalization. When they calm down and stop vocalizing, immediately reward them with praise or treats, reinforcing the behavior you want to see.

At the same time, it's essential to provide an appropriate outlet for self-expression. Pets often bark, meow, or make other noises when they're bored, anxious, or frustrated, so offering them mentally stimulating activities can help reduce the need for excessive vocalization. Interactive play, such as puzzle toys or agility training, gives pets an outlet for their energy and helps them communicate through movement and engagement rather than constant vocalization. These activities also provide an opportunity for pets to feel heard and acknowledged, as they work with you to achieve goals or solve puzzles.

For pets that have difficulty expressing themselves or seem withdrawn, it's crucial to build up their confidence in communication through positive reinforcement. Anytime your pet attempts to communicate—whether through vocalizations, body language, or behavior—respond by acknowledging their efforts and rewarding them with attention or treats. This not only encourages your pet to continue expressing themselves but also helps them understand that their communication is valued and understood.

In addition to positive reinforcement, energy healing practices such as Reiki can be particularly helpful for pets with blocked Throat Chakras. Reiki practitioners can focus specifically on the throat area, channeling healing energy to release emotional or energetic blockages that may be preventing your pet from communicating effectively. Even if you are not trained in Reiki, you can offer your own form of hands-on healing by placing your hands gently on your pet's throat while visualizing a bright blue light radiating from the chakra. This blue light represents the energy of the Throat Chakra, helping to clear any blockages and allowing for freer, more confident expression.

Guided visualizations are another technique that can help balance the Throat Chakra, especially for pets that are sensitive to energy work. Sit with your pet in a quiet, comfortable space, and guide them through a visualization where they imagine their throat opening and releasing any tension or blockages. Picture a calm, blue light expanding from their throat area, filling their entire body with calm, clear energy. This practice not only helps open the Throat Chakra but also creates a calming experience for both you and your pet, strengthening the emotional connection between you.

In pets that have experienced trauma or emotional distress, the Throat Chakra can often become blocked due to fear of expression. For example, a pet that has been in a neglectful or abusive situation may have learned to suppress their voice, avoiding communication to prevent punishment or negative outcomes. In these cases, flower essences such as Mimulus or Larch can help pets regain confidence in expressing themselves. Mimulus is particularly helpful for pets that are fearful or anxious, while Larch helps build self-esteem and confidence, encouraging pets to use their voice without fear.

Socialization exercises are also important for helping pets that have difficulty communicating with other animals or humans. By gradually exposing your pet to positive social interactions—

whether through playdates, group walks, or simply spending time in new environments—you help them build the confidence to express themselves in various settings. Socialization helps pets learn how to communicate not only with their owners but also with other animals and people, promoting overall emotional well-being and balance in the Throat Chakra.

Dietary support can also play a role in balancing the Throat Chakra, especially for pets with physical issues in the throat or respiratory system. Foods that resonate with the energy of the Throat Chakra—such as blueberries, apples, and other blue or purple fruits—can help energize this area and support healing. For pets, incorporating natural, whole foods into their diet, along with supplements that promote respiratory health, can support both physical and energetic healing of the Throat Chakra.

Lastly, creating a calm, supportive environment is key to maintaining a balanced Throat Chakra. Pets are highly sensitive to their surroundings, and loud, chaotic environments can lead to stress or overexpression. Ensuring that your pet has a quiet space to retreat to, where they can relax and feel secure, helps reduce anxiety and promotes healthy communication. Playing soothing music or nature sounds in your pet's space can also create a calming atmosphere that encourages emotional balance and open communication.

In conclusion, balancing and unblocking the Throat Chakra involves a combination of sound therapy, energy healing, behavioral training, and emotional support. By providing your pet with opportunities to express themselves in a safe, controlled manner, you help them build confidence in their communication abilities, promoting overall emotional well-being. In the next chapter, we will explore the Third Eye Chakra, which governs intuition and perception, and how balancing this chakra can enhance your pet's natural instincts and intuitive abilities.

Chapter 18
Focus on the Third Eye Chakra

The Third Eye Chakra, located between the eyes on the forehead, is the center of intuition, perception, and mental clarity in both humans and animals. For pets, this chakra governs their natural instincts, the ability to sense unseen energies, and their connection to their surroundings on a deeper level. A balanced Third Eye Chakra allows pets to tap into their intuitive abilities, make quick, confident decisions, and trust their instincts, leading to improved behavior, greater emotional stability, and an overall sense of well-being. When this chakra is blocked or imbalanced, pets may exhibit confusion, anxiety, and difficulty following their instincts, which can affect their behavior and emotional health.

The Third Eye Chakra is associated with the color indigo and the element of light. It is connected to the mind's eye, which allows animals to perceive the world beyond their immediate physical senses. This chakra plays a vital role in animals' ability to understand their environment, process information, and respond to subtle energy shifts. A pet with a balanced Third Eye Chakra demonstrates keen awareness, alertness, and adaptability, responding to stimuli with clarity and purpose. In contrast, a blocked or overactive Third Eye Chakra may cause pets to become either overly cautious or disconnected, leading to anxiety, fear, or confusion in their daily lives.

An underactive Third Eye Chakra can manifest as a lack of trust in instincts. Pets may appear uncertain or hesitant in new situations, display signs of fear or anxiety, or seem generally disconnected from their surroundings. They may struggle to adapt to changes or rely too heavily on their owners for direction, rather than trusting their natural instincts. In some cases, an underactive Third Eye Chakra can result in physical symptoms such as eye or vision problems, headaches, or neurological imbalances, as the flow of energy to this center is disrupted.

Conversely, an overactive Third Eye Chakra can cause pets to become hyper-aware, leading to anxiety or overreactions to stimuli. These pets may be overly sensitive to changes in their environment, reacting intensely to small noises, movements, or energy shifts. They might exhibit heightened alertness, constant pacing, or an inability to relax. This state of heightened awareness can be overwhelming for pets, causing them to feel restless or anxious, as they struggle to process the constant flow of sensory information.

To begin balancing the Third Eye Chakra, it is essential to help pets develop trust in their own instincts and improve their mental clarity. One of the most effective ways to balance this chakra is through guided visualization exercises, which help pets strengthen their intuitive connection to their environment. These exercises involve creating a calm, meditative space where both you and your pet can relax. Sit quietly with your pet and guide them through a visualization where they imagine a soft, indigo light glowing between their eyes. This light represents the energy of the Third Eye Chakra, and as it grows brighter, it helps clear away any confusion or uncertainty, allowing your pet to feel more grounded and intuitive.

Crystal therapy can also be used to support the healing of the Third Eye Chakra. Stones such as amethyst, lapis lazuli, and sodalite resonate with the energy of this chakra and can help enhance intuition and mental clarity. Amethyst is particularly effective for calming overactive energy in the Third Eye Chakra, helping pets that are anxious or overly sensitive to relax and trust their instincts. Lapis lazuli promotes mental clarity and awareness, making it useful for pets that struggle with decision-making or seem disconnected from their surroundings. Sodalite supports emotional balance and can help pets integrate their intuitive abilities into their daily lives.

To use crystals for Third Eye Chakra healing, you can place them near your pet's resting area or gently lay them on their forehead while they relax. You can also create a crystal grid around your pet's bed or favorite spot, setting the intention for mental clarity, intuition, and inner calm. If your pet is comfortable with touch, you can hold a crystal in your hand and lightly stroke their forehead, visualizing the healing energy flowing into their Third Eye Chakra.

Sound therapy is another powerful tool for balancing the Third Eye Chakra, especially for pets that are sensitive to energy shifts or environmental stimuli. The sound associated with the Third Eye Chakra is "Om," and playing or chanting this sound can help calm overactive energy and restore balance. Instruments such as Tibetan bowls or chimes that produce resonant tones in the key of A, which corresponds to the Third Eye Chakra, can also be used to create a soothing atmosphere that promotes mental clarity and intuition. Playing these sounds near your pet during meditation or relaxation helps to clear any blockages in the Third Eye Chakra and allows your pet to connect more deeply with their intuitive abilities.

For pets that struggle with mental clarity or confusion, incorporating training exercises that encourage decision-making can help strengthen their confidence and trust in their instincts. Simple activities such as choosing between different toys, finding hidden treats, or navigating obstacle courses allow pets to use their problem-solving skills and intuition. These exercises help pets build trust in their own abilities, promoting a more balanced and confident approach to decision-making.

Aromatherapy can also support the healing of the Third Eye Chakra. Essential oils such as frankincense, sandalwood, and lavender are known for their calming and clarifying properties and can help reduce anxiety while promoting mental focus. Diffusing these oils in your pet's environment creates a peaceful atmosphere that encourages relaxation and clarity. You can also apply diluted oils to your pet's forehead, where the Third Eye Chakra is located, to directly stimulate this energy center.

For pets that experience anxiety or overreaction to stimuli, it is important to create a calm, supportive environment where they can feel safe and secure. Reducing external stimuli, such as loud noises or sudden movements, can help prevent overstimulation of the Third Eye Chakra. Offering your pet a quiet, comfortable space where they can retreat and relax helps them reset their energy and avoid becoming overwhelmed by their surroundings.

Mindfulness exercises can also be beneficial for pets with overactive Third Eye Chakras. Teaching your pet to stay present in the moment through focused activities, such as slow, mindful walks or gentle touch, helps them ground their energy and reduce mental overstimulation. During these activities, encourage your pet to focus on their surroundings, using their senses to explore the sights, sounds, and smells around them. This practice not only promotes relaxation but also helps pets develop a stronger connection to their environment, improving their intuitive abilities.

For pets that have experienced trauma or emotional distress, the Third Eye Chakra may become blocked as a result of fear or mistrust. These pets may struggle to trust their own instincts or feel disconnected from their environment. In these cases, Reiki or other forms of energy healing can be particularly effective. Reiki practitioners can focus on the Third Eye Chakra, channeling healing energy to release any emotional or energetic blockages that may be preventing your pet from fully connecting with their intuitive abilities. Even if you are not a trained Reiki practitioner, you can offer your own form of energy healing by placing your hands gently on your pet's forehead and visualizing a calming indigo light surrounding the area. This light represents the energy of the Third Eye Chakra, helping to clear away any confusion or fear and restore balance.

Dietary support can also play a role in balancing the Third Eye Chakra. Incorporating foods that resonate with the energy of this chakra—such as blueberries, blackberries, and purple vegetables—into your pet's diet can help energize this area and support mental clarity. For pets, a natural, whole-food diet that promotes overall health and vitality can also support the flow of energy to the Third Eye Chakra, ensuring that your pet has the physical and energetic resources they need to stay grounded and connected.

Lastly, maintaining a balanced routine of mental stimulation and relaxation is key to supporting a healthy Third Eye Chakra. Pets thrive on consistency, and creating a predictable schedule that includes moments of quiet reflection, as well as opportunities for exploration and play, helps them stay mentally clear and emotionally balanced. Offering regular opportunities for your pet to engage with their environment in a calm, controlled manner allows them to build trust in their instincts while avoiding overstimulation.

Balancing the Third Eye Chakra is essential for promoting mental clarity, intuition, and emotional stability in pets. By using techniques such as guided visualization, crystal therapy, sound healing, and mindfulness exercises, you can help your pet connect more deeply with their intuitive abilities and trust their instincts. In the next chapter, we will explore more advanced techniques for stimulating and opening the Third Eye Chakra, with a focus on enhancing your pet's perception and intuitive connection to their environment.

To deepen the process of balancing and stimulating the Third Eye Chakra, it's important to integrate more advanced techniques that further enhance your pet's intuitive abilities and perception. The Third Eye Chakra not only governs instinctual responses but also allows animals to perceive energies beyond the physical, fostering a deep connection to their environment, other animals, and their human companions. In this chapter, we will explore practices that help your pet fine-tune their intuition, as well as ways to address deeper energetic blockages that may hinder their ability to fully engage with the world around them.

One of the most powerful methods for deepening the connection to the Third Eye Chakra is through visualization and meditation practices that encourage mental clarity and focus. Pets are highly sensitive to the energy and intentions of their owners, and engaging in a joint meditation session can help strengthen your pet's intuitive abilities while promoting relaxation and balance. Find a quiet space where you and your pet can sit comfortably. Close your eyes and visualize a calm, indigo light glowing at the center of your pet's forehead, just between their eyes. Imagine this light slowly expanding outward, filling the entire space with peaceful energy.

As you hold this visualization, encourage your pet to relax and connect to the energy of the space. Even if your pet doesn't actively participate, the energy you create during this meditation can have a profound calming effect, helping to open and energize their Third Eye Chakra. Pets, especially those that are more intuitive by nature, will often respond to this energy shift by becoming calmer and more focused. Over time, regular meditation sessions can help deepen your pet's connection to their intuition, allowing them to tap into their natural instincts with greater ease.

Reiki and other forms of energy healing are also particularly effective for unblocking and stimulating the Third Eye Chakra at a deeper level. For pets that have experienced trauma, fear, or confusion, these energy healing practices can help release energetic blockages that prevent them from fully connecting with their intuition. Reiki practitioners often focus on the Third Eye Chakra during healing sessions, using specific hand positions and visualizations to channel healing energy into this area. By clearing away stagnant or blocked energy, Reiki helps restore balance and promotes mental clarity.

Even if you are not trained in energy healing, you can perform a simple hands-on energy practice with your pet. Sit quietly with your pet and gently place your hand on their forehead, just between their eyes where the Third Eye Chakra is located. As you hold your hand there, imagine a soothing, indigo light flowing from your hand into your pet's Third Eye Chakra, clearing away any blockages and allowing for a free flow of energy. This practice not only helps balance the Third Eye Chakra but also strengthens the bond between you and your pet, as your pet will sense your intention and energy.

For pets that are prone to overreaction or anxiety, it's important to integrate grounding exercises alongside Third Eye Chakra stimulation. Pets with an overactive Third Eye Chakra may become overwhelmed by sensory input, reacting intensely to subtle changes in their environment or becoming overly alert. In these cases, grounding exercises such as slow, mindful walks in nature can help anchor your pet's energy, allowing them to process their surroundings in a calmer, more controlled way. During these walks, encourage your pet to engage with their environment by sniffing the ground, exploring different textures, or listening to the sounds around them. This practice helps them stay present in the moment, reducing overstimulation and promoting mental clarity.

Crystals continue to play a significant role in stimulating the Third Eye Chakra at a deeper level. In addition to amethyst and lapis lazuli, which promote intuition and mental clarity, fluorite is another powerful crystal that can be used to enhance your pet's intuitive abilities. Fluorite is known for its ability to clear mental fog, promote focus, and stimulate the Third Eye Chakra, making it an ideal stone for pets that struggle with decision-making or that seem disconnected from their environment.

To work with fluorite, place the crystal near your pet's bed or favorite resting spot, or gently lay it on their forehead during a relaxation session. You can also create a crystal grid around your pet's resting area using a combination of fluorite, amethyst, and clear quartz to amplify the healing energy and promote a deeper connection to the Third Eye Chakra. As you set up the grid, visualize the crystals working together to clear any blockages and enhance your pet's intuitive abilities.

Sound therapy can also be used to further stimulate the Third Eye Chakra, especially for pets that are highly responsive to sound. Instruments such as tuning forks, Tibetan bowls, or chimes that resonate with the frequency of the Third Eye Chakra (the key of A) can help create a peaceful environment that promotes mental clarity and intuition. You can play these sounds softly in the background during relaxation or meditation sessions with your pet, allowing the vibrations to clear away any stagnant energy in the Third Eye Chakra. The sound "Om" is particularly effective for stimulating this chakra, and you can chant or play recordings of this sound to help activate and balance your pet's intuitive energy.

For pets that seem particularly disconnected or fearful, it's important to build their confidence through activities that encourage them to trust their instincts. Simple decision-making exercises such as choosing between different toys, finding hidden treats, or solving interactive puzzles can help pets strengthen their problem-solving abilities and build trust in their intuition. These activities not only stimulate mental clarity but also provide an outlet for pets to engage with their environment in a meaningful way, promoting balance in the Third Eye Chakra.

For pets that have experienced past trauma or emotional distress, the Third Eye Chakra may be blocked by fear or mistrust. In these cases, flower essences such as Aspen or Cerato can be helpful. Aspen is known for its ability to soothe fears and promote a sense of security, while Cerato helps build self-trust and confidence, encouraging pets to rely on their own intuition rather than seeking constant reassurance from their owners. These essences can be added to your pet's water or administered directly, helping to support emotional healing and restore balance to the Third Eye Chakra.

Guided visualizations can also be a powerful tool for pets with blocked Third Eye Chakras, especially those that struggle with fear or confusion. During a quiet moment, guide your pet through a visualization where they imagine a bright, indigo light glowing at the center of their forehead. As this light expands, it clears away any fear, confusion, or uncertainty, allowing your pet to feel more confident and connected to their instincts. This practice not only helps unblock the Third Eye Chakra but also creates a calming experience that promotes emotional healing and mental clarity.

Aromatherapy can further support the stimulation of the Third Eye Chakra. Essential oils such as frankincense, sandalwood, and lavender are particularly effective for promoting mental clarity and reducing anxiety. You can diffuse these oils in your pet's environment, or apply diluted oils to their forehead to directly stimulate the Third Eye Chakra. These calming scents help create a peaceful atmosphere that encourages your pet to relax and connect with their intuitive abilities.

Lastly, maintaining a balanced routine that includes both mental stimulation and periods of rest is essential for supporting a healthy Third Eye Chakra. Pets thrive on predictability, and offering regular opportunities for relaxation, play, and exploration helps them stay mentally clear and emotionally balanced. Providing moments of quiet reflection, where your pet can rest in a calm, supportive environment, allows them to recharge their energy and avoid overstimulation.

In conclusion, stimulating the Third Eye Chakra involves a combination of visualization, crystal therapy, sound healing, and activities that promote mental clarity and intuitive connection. By helping your pet trust their instincts and engage with their environment in a meaningful way, you can support their emotional and mental well-being, allowing them to live a more balanced and harmonious life. In the next chapter, we will focus on the Crown Chakra, the center of spiritual connection, and explore how balancing this chakra can promote a sense of peace and unity in your pet's life.

Chapter 19
Focus on the Crown Chakra

The Crown Chakra, located at the top of the head, is the energy center responsible for spiritual connection and a sense of unity with the world. In both humans and animals, this chakra governs the feeling of peace, serenity, and alignment with universal energy. For pets, a balanced Crown Chakra promotes calmness, a strong bond with their surroundings, and an overall sense of well-being. When the Crown Chakra is balanced, pets exhibit an inner calm, an openness to their environment, and a deep connection with those around them. However, when this chakra is blocked or imbalanced, it can lead to feelings of restlessness, anxiety, or even disconnection from their surroundings.

The energy of the Crown Chakra is associated with the color violet or white, and it represents the purest form of consciousness. In pets, this chakra helps them feel aligned not only with their environment but also with their human companions and other animals. A pet with a balanced Crown Chakra will demonstrate trust, calmness, and a sense of security, even in unfamiliar situations. On the other hand, an underactive Crown Chakra can manifest as isolation or fear of engaging with their surroundings, while an overactive Crown Chakra may lead to overstimulation, restlessness, or an inability to relax.

To begin balancing the Crown Chakra, it's essential to create an environment that promotes peace and stillness. A calm, serene atmosphere allows the pet's energy to align with the higher frequencies associated with this chakra. Start by designating a quiet space in your home where your pet can retreat and relax. This space should be free from distractions, loud noises, or sudden movements, allowing your pet to feel safe and at ease.

You can enhance this environment by using soft, ambient lighting, preferably in violet or white tones, which resonate with the energy of the Crown Chakra. Additionally, incorporating natural elements such as plants, crystals, or calming scents can help ground your pet's energy and promote serenity.

One of the most effective ways to balance the Crown Chakra is through Reiki or other forms of energy healing. Reiki practitioners can focus on the Crown Chakra by channeling healing energy directly into this area, clearing away any blockages and restoring balance. During a Reiki session, the practitioner may place their hands gently on or near the pet's head, visualizing a stream of white or violet light flowing into the Crown Chakra. This light helps to open and energize the chakra, allowing the pet to feel more connected to their environment and experience a sense of inner peace.

Even if you are not trained in Reiki, you can offer your own form of hands-on healing by placing your hands gently on your pet's head while they are in a relaxed state. As you hold your hands in place, imagine a bright white or violet light flowing from your hands into your pet's Crown Chakra, clearing away any stagnant energy and promoting balance. This practice not only helps to balance the Crown Chakra but also strengthens the bond between you and your pet, as your pet will sense the calming energy and intention behind your touch.

Crystal therapy is another powerful tool for balancing the Crown Chakra. Crystals such as amethyst, clear quartz, and selenite resonate strongly with the energy of this chakra and can be used to promote spiritual connection and inner peace. Amethyst is particularly effective for calming the mind and promoting a sense of serenity, while clear quartz amplifies energy and helps clear blockages in the Crown Chakra. Selenite, with its high vibrational energy, can be used to purify and open the Crown Chakra, allowing for a deeper connection to universal energy.

To use crystals for Crown Chakra healing, place them near your pet's bed or favorite resting spot, or gently lay them on your pet's head while they relax. You can also create a crystal grid around your pet's resting area using a combination of amethyst, clear quartz, and selenite to amplify the healing energy. As you set up the grid, visualize the crystals working together to clear any blockages and enhance your pet's connection to their spiritual energy.

Guided meditation is also highly beneficial for balancing the Crown Chakra, particularly when combined with visualization techniques. Sit quietly with your pet in a calm environment and guide them through a meditation where you both visualize a soft, white light glowing at the top of their head. As this light expands, imagine it filling their entire body with peaceful, calming energy, allowing your pet to feel more connected and aligned with their surroundings. This visualization not only helps to clear any blockages in the Crown Chakra but also promotes a deep sense of serenity and relaxation.

Aromatherapy can further support the balancing of the Crown Chakra. Essential oils such as lavender, frankincense, and myrrh are known for their calming and grounding properties and can help promote a sense of spiritual connection and inner peace. You can diffuse these oils in your pet's environment, or apply diluted oils to their head or neck to directly stimulate the Crown Chakra. The soothing scents help create a peaceful atmosphere that encourages your pet to relax and align with their spiritual energy.

For pets that seem disconnected or restless, it's important to offer activities that promote calmness and help ground their energy. Slow, mindful walks in nature can be particularly effective for pets with an overactive Crown Chakra, as the natural environment helps ground their energy and allows them to connect with the earth. During these walks, encourage your pet to engage with their surroundings by sniffing the ground, exploring different textures, or listening to the sounds of nature. This practice helps anchor their energy and prevents overstimulation, allowing them to process their environment in a more balanced way.

For pets that struggle with fear or anxiety, the Crown Chakra may be blocked by feelings of insecurity or disconnection. In these cases, flower essences such as Vervain or Aspen can be helpful. Vervain promotes inner peace and calmness, while Aspen helps soothe fears and encourage a sense of security. These essences can be added to your pet's water or administered directly, helping to support emotional healing and restore balance to the Crown Chakra.

Mindfulness exercises can also help pets that have difficulty staying present or seem easily distracted. Teaching your pet to focus on simple, repetitive activities—such as gentle brushing, slow feeding rituals, or quiet play—helps them stay grounded in the present moment and reduces mental overstimulation. These exercises not only promote calmness but also allow pets to connect more deeply with their surroundings, fostering a sense of peace and balance in the Crown Chakra.

In addition to these practices, maintaining a balanced routine that includes regular periods of rest and relaxation is key to supporting a healthy Crown Chakra. Pets thrive on consistency, and providing regular opportunities for quiet reflection, play, and exploration helps them stay mentally clear and emotionally balanced. Offering moments of quiet solitude, where your pet can rest in a calm, supportive environment, allows them to recharge their energy and maintain a sense of inner peace.

Dietary support can also play a role in balancing the Crown Chakra. Incorporating foods that resonate with the energy of this chakra—such as purple or white fruits and vegetables—into your pet's diet can help energize this area and support their overall well-being. For pets, a natural, whole-food diet that promotes physical health and vitality can also support the flow of energy to the Crown Chakra, ensuring that your pet has the physical and energetic resources they need to stay grounded and connected.

Balancing the Crown Chakra involves a combination of energy healing, meditation, crystal therapy, and activities that promote calmness and spiritual connection. By helping your pet connect more deeply with their surroundings and promoting a sense of peace and serenity, you can support their emotional and mental well-being, allowing them to live a more balanced and harmonious life. In the next chapter, we will explore more advanced techniques for fully opening and aligning the Crown Chakra, with a focus on helping your pet achieve a deeper state of spiritual connection and inner peace.

In this chapter, we will deepen the exploration of techniques to fully open and align the Crown Chakra in pets. This chakra, being the center of spiritual connection, is essential for fostering a state of inner peace, serenity, and a sense of oneness with the world. When a pet's Crown Chakra is balanced and open, they exhibit calmness, emotional stability, and a harmonious connection with their environment and the beings around them. However, an imbalanced Crown Chakra can lead to feelings of detachment, confusion, or emotional instability. Through advanced practices, we aim to help pets achieve a more profound state of spiritual alignment and well-being.

To begin, one of the most effective ways to open the Crown Chakra is through guided meditations that incorporate visualization techniques. These practices help pets connect with the universal energy surrounding them, clearing any energetic blockages that may have developed. As you sit with your pet in a calm, quiet environment, focus on guiding them through a meditation that emphasizes the flow of spiritual energy into the Crown Chakra. Close your eyes and visualize a pure, bright white or violet light entering your pet's body from the top of their head, flowing down through their entire energy system. As this light flows, it purifies and energizes the Crown Chakra, allowing your pet to experience a sense of lightness, peace, and unity.

During this meditation, you can use Reiki symbols if you are familiar with Reiki practice. The Dai Ko Myo symbol, known as the "Master Symbol," is particularly effective for healing and opening the Crown Chakra. This symbol is associated with deep spiritual healing and can be visualized or drawn in the air above your pet's head as you focus on channeling healing energy. Even if you are not trained in Reiki, you can still create a similar effect by setting a powerful intention to send healing energy to your pet, imagining the white or violet light growing brighter and stronger as it enters their Crown Chakra.

Crystals play a key role in this more advanced stage of balancing the Crown Chakra. While amethyst, clear quartz, and selenite are still important, you can now introduce moonstone or diamond as additional high-vibration stones that resonate with the energy of the Crown Chakra. Moonstone is known for its ability to enhance spiritual connection and intuition, making it particularly useful for pets that may have difficulty engaging with their surroundings or seem disconnected. Diamond—though rare and powerful—offers clarity, amplifies energy, and helps clear any deep blockages in the Crown Chakra.

To use these crystals effectively, you can place them in a circular grid around your pet, with the intention of creating a flow of healing energy that clears and opens the Crown Chakra. Position clear quartz at the center of the grid to amplify the energy, with amethyst, selenite, and moonstone forming a protective circle around it. This configuration helps to focus the energy on the Crown Chakra while promoting a deep sense of spiritual alignment and inner peace.

In addition to crystal grids, placing crystals directly on your pet's body can further enhance the healing process. During moments of rest or relaxation, gently place a piece of clear quartz or selenite on top of your pet's head, where the Crown Chakra is located. This direct contact allows the crystal's energy to interact with the pet's chakra more powerfully, promoting balance and alignment. As your pet rests with the crystal in place, visualize a bright white or violet light expanding from the crystal, filling your pet's entire body with healing energy.

Sound therapy continues to be a powerful tool for balancing the Crown Chakra, particularly when used in more advanced ways. Tibetan bowls, tuning forks, and chimes that resonate with the frequency of the Crown Chakra (often in the key of B) can help create a deep, meditative state that promotes healing and alignment. During a relaxation or meditation session, gently play these instruments near your pet, allowing the sound vibrations to clear away any blockages in the Crown Chakra and promote spiritual connection.

The sound "Om" is especially significant when working with the Crown Chakra, as it represents the vibration of universal energy. Chanting or playing recordings of the "Om" sound while your pet relaxes can help deepen their connection to this energy, allowing them to feel more aligned with the world around them. This practice is particularly beneficial for pets that struggle with feelings of isolation or disconnection, as the sound of "Om" promotes a sense of unity and oneness with the universe.

For pets that are particularly sensitive to energy shifts, it is important to maintain a balance between spiritual connection and grounding. Pets with an overactive Crown Chakra may become overstimulated, leading to restlessness or anxiety. In these cases, grounding exercises, such as slow walks in nature or touch-based bonding activities, can help your pet stay present and calm. Encouraging your pet to connect with the earth through tactile experiences—like sniffing plants, walking on natural surfaces, or engaging in gentle physical contact—helps balance the higher vibrations of the Crown Chakra with the grounding energy of the Root Chakra.

Aromatherapy can be used to support the opening of the Crown Chakra as well. Essential oils like frankincense, sandalwood, and lavender continue to be valuable for promoting a calm and peaceful atmosphere. However, you can also introduce oils such as jasmine or rose, which are known for their ability to open the Crown Chakra and enhance spiritual connection. Diffusing these oils in your pet's environment or applying them (diluted) to their fur can help create a serene atmosphere that promotes inner peace and spiritual alignment.

For pets that have experienced trauma or emotional distress, the Crown Chakra may be deeply blocked, preventing them from feeling connected to their environment or to the people around them. In these cases, incorporating flower essences like white chestnut or star of Bethlehem can help support emotional healing. White chestnut helps calm a restless mind, promoting clarity and peace, while star of Bethlehem is particularly effective for soothing past traumas and encouraging a sense of comfort and safety. These essences can be added to your pet's water or administered directly to support the energetic healing of the Crown Chakra.

Finally, maintaining a consistent routine of spiritual practice is key to keeping the Crown Chakra balanced. Pets, like humans, benefit from regular spiritual engagement, whether it's through energy healing sessions, meditative walks, or quiet moments of reflection. By incorporating these practices into your daily routine, you help your pet stay connected to their spiritual energy while promoting a sense of calm and inner peace. Regular moments of stillness and mindfulness not only benefit the Crown Chakra but also help balance the entire energy system, ensuring that your pet remains centered and aligned.

In conclusion, opening and balancing the Crown Chakra in pets involves a combination of advanced energy healing techniques, meditation, crystal therapy, sound therapy, and aromatherapy. By helping your pet connect with their higher spiritual energy and promoting inner peace, you can support their emotional and mental well-being, allowing them to live a more balanced and harmonious life. In the next chapter, we will explore the power of sound therapy, focusing on how vibrational frequencies can be used to promote healing and balance throughout your pet's entire energetic system.

Chapter 20
Vibrational Frequencies for Healing

Sound therapy is a powerful tool in holistic healing, known for its ability to influence not just the physical body but also the emotional and energetic well-being of animals. For pets, sound therapy can promote relaxation, balance their energy centers, and aid in healing various ailments. Sound resonates with the natural frequencies of the body and mind, and when used thoughtfully, it can calm the nervous system, release stress, and restore equilibrium in pets, much like it does in humans.

Animals are particularly sensitive to sound and vibrational frequencies. Their acute hearing and heightened awareness of their environment mean that sounds can have a profound effect on their well-being, whether calming or agitating. This makes it crucial to use the right sounds and frequencies when incorporating sound therapy into a holistic healing regimen. Pets that are anxious, restless, or overstimulated can especially benefit from soothing frequencies, as these sounds help align their energy and promote a sense of calm.

The most common forms of sound therapy include the use of Tibetan singing bowls, chimes, tuning forks, and even healing music designed specifically to address different emotional or energetic states. These instruments and sound sources work by producing sound waves that vibrate at specific frequencies. When these vibrations interact with the energy field of a pet, they can help release blockages, promote relaxation, and harmonize the pet's overall energetic system.

Tibetan singing bowls, for instance, produce deep, resonating sounds that can quickly bring about a state of calm. Their vibrations are particularly effective at influencing the chakras, including those of animals, and can help rebalance energy centers that have become blocked or stagnant. To use a singing bowl with your pet, begin by creating a quiet, peaceful environment. Place the bowl near your pet and gently tap it to create a soft tone. As the bowl vibrates, move it slowly around your pet's body, allowing the sound waves to penetrate their energy field. Pets are usually very receptive to the calming vibrations of a singing bowl, and you'll notice that many pets will begin to relax or even fall asleep during this process.

Another powerful instrument in sound therapy is the tuning fork. Tuning forks produce a pure tone when struck, which resonates at a precise frequency. Different tuning forks are tuned to specific frequencies, often aligned with the chakra system. For example, a tuning fork tuned to the frequency of the Root Chakra can help ground an anxious pet, while one tuned to the frequency of the Crown Chakra can promote peace and spiritual connection. To use a tuning fork, strike it gently against a soft surface to produce the tone, then hold it near your pet's body, focusing on areas where you feel their energy is out of balance. The vibrations from the tuning fork can help realign the energy flow and promote healing.

Chimes and bells are also highly effective tools for sound healing. Their light, airy tones can clear stagnant energy and promote mental clarity and focus. Pets that are lethargic or mentally disconnected may benefit from the gentle ringing of chimes, which can stimulate their energy field and encourage engagement with their environment. Like other sound healing instruments, chimes should be played softly in the presence of your pet, creating a gentle, soothing atmosphere.

One of the key benefits of sound therapy is that it not only addresses physical and emotional imbalances but also helps to harmonize the pet's energetic field. Pets, like humans, have an aura or energy field that extends beyond their physical body. When their aura is out of balance or disrupted—often due to stress, illness, or trauma—sound therapy can help restore harmony by clearing away negative or stagnant energy. This is particularly beneficial for pets that are recovering from surgery, illness, or emotional trauma, as sound therapy can help accelerate the healing process by addressing not just the physical body but the energetic body as well.

In addition to Tibetan bowls and tuning forks, healing music specifically composed for pets can be a valuable tool in sound therapy. This music is designed to resonate with the frequencies that calm the nervous system and promote relaxation in animals. Many pet owners find that playing calming music in the background during stressful situations—such as thunderstorms, vet visits, or when introducing new pets—can help reduce anxiety and create a more peaceful environment. This type of music often incorporates soft, repetitive tones, nature sounds, and slow tempos, which help synchronize the pet's brainwaves with a relaxed state.

It's important to note that when using sound therapy with pets, sensitivity to volume and frequency is essential. Pets, especially dogs and cats, have much more acute hearing than humans, and sounds that are too loud or high-pitched can cause discomfort rather than healing. Always begin with low volumes and gentle tones, observing your pet's reactions to ensure they are comfortable and at ease. Signs that your pet is responding positively to sound therapy include relaxed body posture, deep breathing, and sometimes even sleep.

For pets that are particularly sensitive to sound or new experiences, it's important to introduce sound therapy gradually. Start with short, gentle sessions, allowing your pet to become accustomed to the new sounds and sensations. Over time, as they become more comfortable, you can extend the length of the sessions and introduce new instruments or sounds. Remember to always maintain a calm and reassuring presence during the session, as your energy will influence how your pet responds to the therapy.

Breathwork can complement sound therapy, both for the pet and the owner. As you play the sound healing instruments, focus on your own breathing, taking slow, deep breaths to maintain a calm, centered state. Pets are highly attuned to the emotional and energetic state of their owners, and your calm presence will enhance the effectiveness of the sound therapy. If your pet is particularly anxious, you can also incorporate breathing exercises into the session, encouraging them to relax and synchronize their energy with yours.

Sound therapy can also be combined with other healing modalities, such as Reiki, massage, or aromatherapy, to amplify its effects. For example, playing calming music or using a singing bowl during a Reiki session can help deepen the pet's relaxation and enhance the flow of energy. Similarly, using a tuning fork while performing a gentle massage can help release physical tension and promote healing at a deeper level.

Incorporating sound therapy into your pet's daily routine can have long-lasting benefits. Regular sound healing sessions, even as short as 10 to 15 minutes, can help maintain energetic balance, reduce stress, and support overall well-being. Whether it's playing soft music during quiet times, using a Tibetan bowl to start or end the day, or simply offering a few moments of sound-based relaxation after a stressful event, these practices can help create a harmonious environment for both you and your pet.

Sound therapy is a versatile and powerful tool for promoting physical, emotional, and energetic healing in pets. By using instruments such as Tibetan bowls, tuning forks, and chimes, as well as calming music, you can help restore balance to your pet's energy system, reduce stress, and support their overall well-being. In the next chapter, we will explore more advanced techniques for using sound therapy, including how to combine it with other holistic practices to maximize its healing potential for your pet.

In this chapter, we will explore more advanced techniques for using sound therapy to heal and energize pets. Sound therapy can be combined with other holistic practices to create a powerful, multidimensional healing experience. By understanding how to integrate different sound healing tools with modalities like Reiki, aromatherapy, and crystal therapy, pet owners can promote deeper emotional and energetic balance for their animals.

As we discussed in the previous chapter, sound therapy works by using specific frequencies to influence the body and mind. Each frequency resonates with a different energy center (or chakra) in the body, and pets are no exception. In this chapter, we will look at how different sound frequencies can be used to target specific chakras in your pet's energy system, helping to restore balance and release blockages that may be causing emotional or physical distress.

One of the most powerful ways to amplify the effects of sound therapy is by combining it with Reiki, a form of energy healing. Reiki works by channeling universal energy into the body, promoting relaxation and healing at an energetic level. When combined with sound therapy, the vibrations from the sound healing instruments can enhance the flow of Reiki energy, helping to clear blockages and harmonize the chakras.

To begin a session that integrates sound therapy and Reiki, start by creating a calm, quiet environment for your pet. You can use soft lighting, perhaps with candles or a dimmed lamp, to help set the tone for relaxation. Begin with Reiki, placing your hands gently on or near your pet's body. As you allow Reiki energy to flow, use a Tibetan singing bowl or chimes to create soft, resonating tones that support the energy work. Focus on moving the bowl or chimes around your pet's body, targeting areas where you sense energy blockages or tension.

For example, if your pet seems anxious or fearful, their Root Chakra may be unbalanced. In this case, you can use lower-frequency sounds that resonate with the Root Chakra to help ground and stabilize their energy. Alternatively, if your pet seems emotionally withdrawn or disconnected, you might focus on their Heart Chakra, using mid-range frequencies that promote love, connection, and emotional healing.

Using tuning forks that are tuned to specific chakras can be particularly effective in this context. Strike the fork to produce its tone, then gently move it along your pet's body, holding it over key chakra points to stimulate energy flow. The combination of Reiki energy and sound frequencies creates a synergistic effect, encouraging your pet to release any stuck energy and move towards a state of balance and calm.

Chakras can become blocked or overactive due to stress, trauma, or illness. When this happens, the energy flow through the body becomes disrupted, leading to physical, emotional, or behavioral issues. By using specific sound frequencies, you can help to unblock or balance your pet's chakras, promoting overall well-being.

Each chakra resonates with a different frequency, and by using tuning forks, singing bowls, or even healing music that corresponds to these frequencies, you can target each chakra individually. Here's a breakdown of how to approach chakra healing with sound:

Root Chakra (Muladhara): Located at the base of the spine, this chakra governs feelings of security and grounding. Use lower-frequency sounds, such as drumming or low-pitched singing bowls, to bring balance to this chakra. The sound helps to ground your pet's energy and reduce anxiety or fear.

Sacral Chakra (Svadhisthana): This chakra, located just below the belly button, is associated with emotions and creativity. Use mid-range frequencies or water sounds, which resonate with the fluidity of this chakra, to promote emotional balance.

Solar Plexus Chakra (Manipura): This chakra, located in the abdomen, is connected to personal power and confidence. To energize this chakra, use bright, higher-pitched sounds such as chimes or tuning forks in the key of E.

Heart Chakra (Anahata): Located at the center of the chest, the Heart Chakra governs love and emotional well-being. Use gentle, resonant sounds in the key of F, such as singing bowls or tuning forks, to open and balance this chakra. These sounds help to restore a sense of love and connection, promoting emotional healing.

Throat Chakra (Vishuddha): Responsible for communication and expression, the Throat Chakra resonates with sounds in the key of G. Bells, chimes, or bowls that create clear, pure tones can help unblock this chakra and promote healthy communication in your pet.

Third Eye Chakra (Ajna): Located in the center of the forehead, the Third Eye Chakra is associated with intuition and insight. Use high-pitched frequencies, such as those produced by crystal singing bowls, to stimulate this chakra and encourage mental clarity and intuitive perception.

Crown Chakra (Sahasrara): The highest chakra, located at the top of the head, is connected to spiritual connection and enlightenment. Use the highest-frequency sounds, such as those from tuning forks or singing bowls in the key of B, to promote balance in this chakra. These sounds help open the Crown Chakra, encouraging a deep sense of peace and connection to the universe.

Enhancing Sound Therapy with Crystals and Aromatherapy

To further enhance the healing effects of sound therapy, you can incorporate crystals and aromatherapy into your session. Crystals, which have their own vibrational frequencies, can work in harmony with sound vibrations to amplify the healing effects. For example, placing amethyst or clear quartz crystals around your pet during a sound therapy session can help to deepen their connection to the healing energy, particularly when working on the higher chakras like the Third Eye or Crown.

To combine sound therapy with aromatherapy, diffuse calming essential oils such as lavender, chamomile, or frankincense during the session. The gentle scent of these oils can help your pet relax more deeply, enhancing the overall healing experience. Be sure to use pet-safe essential oils, and avoid using strong scents that may overwhelm your pet's sensitive nose.

Creating a Sound Healing Routine

Incorporating sound therapy into your pet's daily or weekly routine can have profound long-term effects on their well-being. Regular sound healing sessions, even if brief, help to maintain energetic balance, reduce stress, and promote emotional healing. You can create a simple routine that involves playing healing music or using a singing bowl for a few minutes each day, particularly during moments of stress or after stimulating activities.

For pets with chronic anxiety or behavioral issues, regular use of sound therapy can help to retrain their nervous system, gradually reducing their stress response and promoting a calmer, more balanced demeanor. Over time, you may notice improvements in their behavior, energy levels, and overall emotional health.

Sound therapy can be particularly beneficial for pets with specific health conditions, both physical and emotional. For instance:

Anxious or fearful pets benefit from low-frequency sounds that ground their energy and promote relaxation. Use singing bowls or tuning forks in the key of C (Root Chakra) to help them feel more secure and at ease.

Pets recovering from illness or surgery can benefit from mid-range frequencies that energize the body's natural healing processes. Use bowls or chimes that resonate with the Heart and Solar Plexus Chakras to promote recovery and vitality.

Elderly pets may experience physical discomfort and reduced mobility. Sound therapy that focuses on the Root and Sacral Chakras can help ease pain and increase their sense of comfort. Use low-pitched bowls or tuning forks to create a soothing, supportive environment for them.

Integrating Sound Healing with Other Holistic Practices

Sound healing works best when integrated with other holistic treatments, creating a multi-layered approach to your pet's care. For example, you can begin with a sound healing session to relax your pet's energy, followed by a Reiki treatment to further clear energy blockages. Alternatively, you can use sound therapy in combination with massage to help release physical tension while aligning your pet's energy.

Overall, sound therapy is an incredibly versatile and powerful tool for supporting your pet's holistic well-being. Whether used on its own or in combination with other healing practices, it offers a gentle, non-invasive way to promote balance, reduce stress, and enhance your pet's quality of life. In the next chapter, we will explore the natural world of homeopathy for animals, focusing on how homeopathic remedies can be used to address physical and emotional issues, and how these natural therapies can complement other holistic practices.

Chapter 21
Homeopathy for Animals

Homeopathy is a natural and gentle form of medicine that has been used for centuries to treat a wide range of conditions in humans and animals alike. Based on the principle of "like cures like," homeopathy works by stimulating the body's innate healing response through the use of highly diluted substances. These remedies are designed to trigger the animal's vital energy to heal itself, rather than suppress symptoms as many conventional treatments do. Homeopathy is particularly effective in treating chronic conditions, emotional imbalances, and even behavioral issues in pets, offering a holistic alternative that complements other forms of care.

Homeopathic remedies are derived from natural substances such as plants, minerals, and animal products, and are prepared through a process of serial dilution and succussion (vigorous shaking). Despite the extreme dilution, homeopathic remedies are believed to carry the energetic imprint of the original substance, which can stimulate the body's healing processes when given in the correct dosage and form.

The fundamental concept of homeopathy is to treat the individual animal as a whole, rather than focusing solely on symptoms. This means taking into account not just the physical condition but also the pet's emotional state, behavior, and overall constitution. For example, two pets suffering from anxiety may receive different homeopathic remedies, depending on their unique personalities and how their anxiety manifests.

The principle of "like cures like" forms the foundation of homeopathy. It suggests that a substance that causes certain symptoms in a healthy individual can be used to treat those same symptoms in a sick individual. For example, a remedy made from a plant that causes vomiting in large doses might be used to treat an animal suffering from nausea and vomiting, but in a highly diluted form. The idea is that the body will recognize the symptoms and activate its natural healing mechanisms to resolve the imbalance.

When it comes to animals, this approach can be highly effective, especially for pets that have not responded well to conventional treatments. Homeopathic remedies are gentle and have no side effects, making them ideal for long-term use in treating chronic conditions. They are also safe to use alongside other therapies, such as acupuncture, massage, and aromatherapy.

One of the key aspects of homeopathy is the selection of the appropriate remedy for your pet's specific condition. Homeopathic remedies are chosen based on the principle of individualization, which means that the remedy must match not only the physical symptoms but also the emotional and behavioral characteristics of the pet. This process involves a detailed understanding of your pet's health, personality, and environment.

To choose the correct remedy, consider the following factors:

Physical Symptoms: What is the nature of the condition? Is it acute (sudden onset) or chronic (long-standing)? What are the specific symptoms? For example, is your pet showing signs of digestive distress, skin issues, respiratory problems, or joint pain?

Emotional State: How does your pet behave during times of illness or discomfort? Are they more irritable, anxious, or withdrawn than usual? Do they seem fearful, restless, or excessively needy? Emotional states are crucial in determining the right homeopathic remedy.

Behavioral Patterns: Has your pet's behavior changed since the onset of the condition? Are they more aggressive, lethargic, or displaying unusual habits? Behavioral clues can help narrow down the choice of remedy.

Environmental Factors: Consider whether there have been any recent changes in your pet's environment, such as a new home, the introduction of a new pet or family member, or a traumatic event. Environmental stressors can exacerbate physical conditions and influence the choice of homeopathic remedy.

Homeopathic remedies are available in various forms, including tablets, liquids, and granules. When selecting a remedy, it is essential to administer the correct potency (strength) and dosage. The most common potencies for animals are 6C, 30C, and 200C, with higher potencies reserved for more severe or deeply rooted conditions. It is advisable to consult with a trained homeopathic practitioner for guidance on choosing the right remedy and potency for your pet.

There are several homeopathic remedies that are widely used to address common conditions in animals. These remedies have a long history of use in both human and veterinary homeopathy and can be particularly effective when selected based on the individual characteristics of the pet. Here are some of the most commonly used remedies and their indications:

Arnica montana: Arnica is one of the most well-known homeopathic remedies, often used for trauma, injury, and physical pain. It is ideal for pets that have suffered a fall, been involved in an accident, or undergone surgery. Arnica helps reduce swelling, pain, and bruising, and promotes faster healing. It is also useful for treating muscle soreness after intense physical activity.

Aconitum napellus: This remedy is particularly helpful for acute conditions that come on suddenly, often accompanied by anxiety or fear. Aconite is commonly used for shock, fever, or the sudden onset of respiratory or digestive issues. It is ideal for pets that display signs of restlessness, fear, or panic, especially after exposure to cold or stressful events.

Pulsatilla: Pulsatilla is an excellent remedy for animals that are emotionally sensitive and tend to be clingy or needy. It is often used for pets that display symptoms of digestive upset or skin issues, particularly when their condition seems to shift frequently. Pulsatilla is also helpful for pets that are highly emotional and crave attention and affection during times of illness.

Phosphorus: This remedy is beneficial for pets that are easily frightened, particularly by loud noises or sudden changes in their environment. Phosphorus is often used to treat conditions such as respiratory issues, bleeding, or digestive disturbances in pets that tend to be social, affectionate, and easily startled.

Nux vomica: Nux vomica is commonly used for digestive issues, particularly those caused by overeating or exposure to toxins. It is ideal for pets that are irritable or sensitive to touch and may be suffering from constipation, vomiting, or bloating. This remedy can also be used to detoxify the body after exposure to harmful substances.

Silica: Silica is helpful for pets that seem weak or frail, particularly those recovering from illness or surgery. It is often used to treat abscesses, skin conditions, and respiratory issues in animals that seem to lack vitality. Silica helps strengthen the immune system and promotes healing of chronic conditions.

One of the great advantages of homeopathy is that the remedies are easy to administer to pets. The remedies are typically given in small doses, either directly into the pet's mouth or mixed with their food or water. Since homeopathic remedies are odorless and tasteless, pets are usually quite willing to take them without resistance.

For acute conditions, remedies are often given every few hours until improvement is seen. For chronic conditions, remedies may be given once or twice daily over an extended period, depending on the severity of the condition and the pet's response. It is important to monitor your pet closely and adjust the dosage as needed, based on their symptoms and overall well-being.

In addition to administering the remedies, it is essential to observe your pet's behavior and emotional state throughout the treatment process. Homeopathic remedies work by stimulating the body's own healing mechanisms, and it is not uncommon to see a temporary aggravation of symptoms before improvement occurs. This is a sign that the body is responding to the remedy and beginning the healing process.

Homeopathy can be used alongside other holistic treatments, such as Reiki, acupuncture, massage, and aromatherapy, to create a comprehensive healing plan for your pet. Because homeopathy works on an energetic level, it complements these other therapies by supporting the body's natural healing processes and helping to restore balance at both the physical and emotional levels.

In particular, homeopathy can be used to address the underlying emotional and behavioral issues that may be contributing to your pet's condition. For example, a pet that is recovering from surgery may benefit from a combination of Arnica for physical pain and Pulsatilla to address the emotional need for comfort and affection during recovery.

In the next chapter, we will explore more advanced applications of homeopathy for treating complex and chronic conditions in pets. You will learn how to select and combine remedies to create a personalized treatment plan for your pet's unique needs.

In chronic and more complex conditions, homeopathy offers a gentle yet powerful way to restore balance and promote healing in animals. Homeopathic treatments work by addressing not only physical symptoms but also the underlying emotional and energetic imbalances that may contribute to a pet's health issues. This chapter delves into selecting, administering, and combining remedies for chronic and long-standing conditions, offering deeper insights into how homeopathy can be applied to enhance a pet's overall well-being.

When treating chronic conditions in pets, it is essential to look beyond the immediate symptoms and consider the animal's overall constitution, personality, and history of health. Chronic conditions often develop slowly, and they may involve recurring episodes of discomfort or illness that weaken the pet over time. In such cases, homeopathy is ideal because it takes a holistic approach, aiming to strengthen the animal's vitality and address the root cause of the issue rather than simply suppressing symptoms.

In homeopathy, chronic conditions require a more individualized treatment plan than acute cases. The remedy chosen must match the pet's specific set of symptoms, as well as their emotional and behavioral responses. For instance, two dogs with arthritis might receive different remedies depending on whether one is irritable and withdrawn, while the other remains sociable but anxious. The key is to identify the core patterns of imbalance that contribute to the chronic condition and select a remedy that addresses the whole animal, not just the symptoms.

Chronic conditions are those that persist over time, often waxing and waning but never completely resolving without proper treatment. Common chronic conditions in pets include skin allergies, arthritis, digestive issues, respiratory problems, and behavioral concerns such as separation anxiety or aggression. These conditions may have a significant impact on a pet's quality of life and, if left untreated, can lead to further health complications.

Homeopathy excels in treating chronic conditions because it works to stimulate the body's innate healing ability. By selecting remedies that match the pet's individual symptoms, homeopathy helps restore balance at a deep level, allowing the pet's body to heal itself more effectively over time. While results may not be immediate, consistent use of homeopathic remedies can lead to gradual improvements in both physical and emotional well-being, making it a valuable tool for managing long-term health conditions.

The selection of homeopathic remedies for chronic conditions requires careful observation and detailed knowledge of the animal's health history. It is essential to take a comprehensive approach, looking at the pet's current symptoms, personality traits, past illnesses, and any external factors that might be influencing their condition, such as environmental changes or emotional stress.

To choose the right remedy for a chronic condition, consider the following aspects:

Physical Symptoms: Observe the specific physical symptoms associated with the condition. For example, in arthritis, note whether the pet is stiff in the morning, favors a particular side of the body, or shows signs of inflammation in specific joints. Chronic skin conditions may involve recurring itching, redness, or hot spots. Detailed symptom observation is key to finding the appropriate remedy.

Emotional and Behavioral Changes: Chronic conditions often affect the pet's emotional state and behavior. For instance, a pet with chronic pain may become more irritable, withdrawn, or anxious. Alternatively, some pets may seek more attention and comfort when dealing with a long-term condition. These emotional responses are important clues in determining the best homeopathic remedy.

Environmental and Lifestyle Factors: Changes in the pet's environment, diet, or daily routine can influence chronic conditions. Consider whether there have been any significant changes in the household, such as a move, the introduction of a new family member, or changes in the pet's diet or exercise routine. Homeopathy seeks to address the totality of the pet's circumstances, so these factors must be considered in the remedy selection process.

Previous Treatment History: Review the pet's history of treatments, including any previous use of homeopathic remedies, conventional medications, or other holistic therapies. Understanding how the pet has responded to past treatments can guide the current remedy selection and ensure that the new treatment plan complements their overall health strategy.

Homeopathy offers a wide range of remedies that can be tailored to treat various chronic conditions in pets. Below are some commonly used remedies for specific conditions, along with their indications:

Rhus toxicodendron: This remedy is often used for arthritis and joint pain, particularly when the pet is stiff upon waking but improves with movement. It is ideal for pets that seem restless at night and seek warmth or stretching to relieve discomfort. Rhus tox helps reduce stiffness and inflammation in the joints, making it useful for chronic musculoskeletal issues.

Sulphur: Sulphur is commonly used to treat chronic skin conditions, especially when there is redness, itching, and dryness. It is beneficial for pets that frequently scratch or lick affected areas, causing irritation or secondary infections. Sulphur is often indicated when the skin condition worsens in heat or after bathing.

Calcarea carbonica: This remedy is ideal for pets that are sluggish, overweight, or prone to digestive issues. It is often used for pets with chronic conditions like obesity, sluggish metabolism, or persistent digestive upsets. Calcarea carb is also useful for pets that become easily fatigued or show signs of weakness, helping to restore vitality and balance.

Silica: Silica is a key remedy for chronic infections, abscesses, and slow-healing wounds. It is particularly helpful for pets that seem weak or prone to recurring infections. Silica helps stimulate the immune system and aids in the expulsion of foreign bodies or toxins, making it ideal for pets with chronic skin infections or abscesses.

Ignatia: Ignatia is often used to treat chronic emotional conditions, particularly those related to grief, separation anxiety, or loss. It is indicated for pets that exhibit signs of emotional distress, such as whimpering, restlessness, or changes in appetite and behavior. Ignatia helps calm the nervous system and restore emotional balance.

Lycopodium: Lycopodium is used for chronic digestive issues, particularly those related to bloating, gas, and liver dysfunction. It is suitable for pets that seem irritable, anxious, or sensitive to changes in their environment. Lycopodium helps improve digestion and liver function, making it useful for pets with chronic gastrointestinal problems.

When treating chronic conditions, homeopathic remedies are usually given less frequently than in acute cases, but over a more extended period. The goal is to stimulate the body's healing response gradually, allowing the pet to regain balance over time.

Remedies may be given once a day or even less frequently, depending on the severity of the condition and the pet's response.

It is important to monitor your pet closely during treatment and adjust the remedy as needed. Some pets may show a temporary aggravation of symptoms before improvement occurs, which is a sign that the remedy is working and the body is beginning to heal. If symptoms worsen or persist without improvement, consult a homeopathic practitioner for guidance on modifying the treatment plan.

In chronic cases, it is also helpful to combine homeopathy with other holistic practices to support the pet's overall well-being. For example, a pet with chronic arthritis might benefit from a combination of homeopathy, acupuncture, and massage therapy to address both the physical and emotional aspects of their condition. Integrating multiple therapies can enhance the effectiveness of homeopathy and provide comprehensive support for long-term healing.

For pets with chronic conditions, it is essential to create a personalized treatment plan that takes into account their unique health needs, personality, and environment. This may involve using a combination of remedies to address different aspects of the condition or adjusting the treatment as the pet's symptoms change over time.

Keep a record of your pet's progress throughout the treatment process, noting any changes in symptoms, behavior, and overall health. This will help you track the effectiveness of the remedies and make informed decisions about any adjustments that may be needed. Over time, as the pet's condition improves, the frequency of remedies can often be reduced, allowing the pet to maintain balance with minimal intervention.

Homeopathy offers a safe and gentle approach to treating chronic conditions in pets, providing long-term relief and promoting overall wellness. By focusing on the pet's individual needs and addressing both physical and emotional imbalances, homeopathy can help pets lead healthier, happier lives.

In the next chapter, we will explore reflexology for animals, a holistic practice that involves stimulating specific points on the paws to promote healing and well-being. This ancient practice complements other therapies, helping to restore balance in the body through gentle pressure techniques.

Chapter 22
Reflexology for Animals: Healing Through Feet and Paws

Reflexology, an ancient practice rooted in Traditional Chinese Medicine, focuses on the application of pressure to specific points on the body, often on the feet, hands, or ears. In animals, the paws are the most accessible and responsive areas for reflexology treatments, and the results can be deeply impactful on their overall health. By stimulating particular reflex points on a pet's paws, we can address imbalances in different organs and systems, promoting relaxation, reducing stress, and supporting healing processes in the body. Reflexology is particularly beneficial for animals because it is gentle, non-invasive, and works in harmony with the body's natural healing mechanisms.

The theory behind reflexology is based on the idea that specific points on the paws correspond to various organs and systems in the body. When pressure is applied to these points, it stimulates energy flow, improves circulation, and enhances the body's ability to heal itself. Reflexology is often used in combination with other holistic treatments, such as massage, aromatherapy, or energy healing, to create a comprehensive approach to well-being.

In this chapter, we will explore the basics of reflexology for pets, focusing on how to map the reflex points on an animal's paws and the techniques required to apply pressure effectively. By the end of the chapter, you will have the knowledge and tools needed to begin integrating reflexology into your pet's wellness routine.

Reflex points are specific areas on the paws that correspond to different parts of the body. For example, the tips of the toes may represent the head and brain, while the center of the paw pad can be linked to internal organs such as the stomach, liver, and kidneys. When pressure is applied to these points, it helps release tension, improve circulation, and support the function of the corresponding organ or system.

Reflexology is known for its ability to reduce stress and promote relaxation, which can be especially important for pets that suffer from anxiety, behavioral issues, or chronic pain. In addition to calming the nervous system, reflexology helps boost circulation and stimulate the lymphatic system, aiding in detoxification and the removal of waste products from the body. These effects make reflexology an excellent supportive treatment for pets with chronic conditions such as arthritis, digestive problems, or respiratory issues.

One of the key benefits of reflexology is that it works with the body's natural healing abilities. Unlike some more invasive treatments, reflexology gently encourages the body to restore balance on its own. This makes it ideal for pets of all ages and health conditions, as it can be tailored to meet the individual needs of each animal without causing discomfort or stress.

To apply reflexology effectively, it is essential to understand the basic reflex points on your pet's paws and how they correspond to different areas of the body. While the exact mapping may vary slightly depending on the size and shape of your pet's paws, the general principles remain consistent.

Here is a simplified guide to the main reflex points on a pet's paw:

Toes: The toes represent the head, neck, and upper part of the body, including the brain, eyes, ears, and sinuses. Applying gentle pressure to the toes can help with conditions related to the nervous system, headaches, sinus issues, and tension in the neck and shoulders.

Paw Pads: The central pad of the paw corresponds to the chest, heart, and lungs. Reflexology on this area can support respiratory health, cardiovascular function, and immune system strength. The sides of the paw pads are linked to the digestive organs, such as the stomach, intestines, liver, and pancreas.

Stimulating these points helps promote digestion and detoxification, making it useful for pets with gastrointestinal issues.

Heel of the Paw: The heel area represents the lower abdomen and pelvic region, including the kidneys, bladder, and reproductive organs. Reflexology on the heel is often used to support urinary health, address hormonal imbalances, and help with reproductive issues.

Claws and Nail Beds: The base of the claws is linked to the limbs, joints, and skeletal system. Massaging this area can help alleviate stiffness, arthritis, and joint pain, particularly in older pets or those with mobility challenges.

Between the Toes: The area between the toes corresponds to the lymphatic system and is associated with detoxification and immune support. Reflexology in this area helps stimulate lymph flow, encouraging the elimination of toxins from the body and boosting the immune system.

Before starting a reflexology session with your pet, it is important to create a calm and relaxed environment. Choose a quiet space where your pet feels comfortable, and ensure that you have enough time to work slowly and gently without rushing the process. Reflexology should always be performed when your pet is calm, as stress or anxiety may make it more difficult for them to relax and benefit from the treatment.

Start by gently massaging your pet's paws to help them relax and get used to the sensation of touch. Some pets may be more sensitive to having their paws handled, especially if they are not accustomed to it, so take your time and work gradually. If your pet seems resistant or uncomfortable, stop and try again later when they are more relaxed.

You can also use calming techniques, such as playing soft music or diffusing essential oils, to create a soothing atmosphere. Essential oils like lavender, chamomile, or frankincense are known for their calming properties and can help your pet feel more at ease during the session. However, always ensure that the oils are diluted properly and safe for use around animals, especially if using them topically.

Once your pet is calm and relaxed, you can begin applying reflexology techniques to their paws. Reflexology is all about gentle pressure and slow movements, so avoid pressing too hard or causing discomfort. The goal is to stimulate the reflex points without causing pain or stress to your pet.

Thumb Walking: One of the most common techniques used in reflexology is called "thumb walking." This involves using the pad of your thumb to apply gentle pressure as you move along the reflex points on the paw. Start at the top of the paw and work your way down, applying steady but light pressure to each area. You can also use your index finger for smaller areas, such as the toes or spaces between the toes.

Circular Motion: In addition to thumb walking, circular motions are often used to stimulate reflex points. Place your thumb or finger on the desired reflex point and make small, slow circles. This helps increase circulation and release tension in the corresponding area of the body.

Hold and Release: Another technique is to apply firm pressure to a reflex point and then release it gradually. Hold the pressure for a few seconds, then gently lift your thumb or finger. This technique can be especially effective for stimulating deeper reflex points or areas that require more focused attention.

Stretching the Toes: Gently stretching your pet's toes can help relieve tension and promote relaxation. Hold each toe between your thumb and forefinger and gently pull it away from the paw, stretching it slightly. This helps open up energy pathways and can be particularly beneficial for pets with tension in the neck or upper body.

Paying Attention to Sensitivity: As you work on your pet's paws, pay attention to any areas that seem particularly sensitive or tender. These areas may indicate imbalances or blockages in the corresponding part of the body. If you notice sensitivity, spend extra time working on those reflex points, but be gentle and monitor your pet's reactions closely. If they show signs of discomfort, reduce the pressure or take a break.

Reflexology can be used as a preventative measure to maintain your pet's health and well-being, or as part of a treatment plan for specific health issues. Some of the most common reasons to use reflexology include:

Reducing stress and anxiety: Reflexology is excellent for calming the nervous system and promoting relaxation, making it ideal for pets that experience anxiety, especially in stressful situations like vet visits, thunderstorms, or separation from their owners.

Supporting chronic conditions: Reflexology can be particularly beneficial for pets with chronic health issues such as arthritis, digestive problems, or respiratory conditions. It helps improve circulation, reduce inflammation, and promote the body's natural healing abilities.

Enhancing overall well-being: Regular reflexology sessions can support your pet's immune system, improve their energy levels, and maintain a healthy balance in their organs and systems. It is a gentle way to enhance their overall quality of life, especially as they age.

In the next chapter, we will explore advanced techniques in reflexology, focusing on how to use this practice to address specific health concerns and integrate it into a broader holistic treatment plan for your pet. We will also discuss how reflexology can be combined with other therapies, such as massage and energy healing, to create a comprehensive approach to healing and well-being.

Building on the basic principles of reflexology introduced in the previous chapter, this section will delve deeper into how to apply reflexology for specific health and behavioral issues in animals. While reflexology can promote overall relaxation and well-being, it can also be tailored to address certain conditions like digestive problems, joint pain, and stress-related behaviors. This chapter will focus on advanced techniques and combinations of reflexology with other holistic practices to enhance its therapeutic effects.

Reflexology can be integrated into a regular wellness routine or used as a targeted therapy when addressing specific ailments. The ability to customize treatments based on your pet's unique needs makes it a versatile tool in holistic health. We will also explore how reflexology can be effectively combined with practices like aromatherapy, Reiki, and massage, amplifying its effects and creating a more comprehensive healing experience.

While the basic techniques of reflexology involve thumb walking, circular motions, and light pressure on reflex points, advanced techniques involve more focused, intentional pressure and attention to areas that may show signs of imbalance. By identifying sensitive or tender areas during a reflexology session, you can determine which systems or organs may need additional support. Below are a few common health concerns in pets that can be alleviated through reflexology:

Digestive Issues: Pets suffering from digestive discomfort, such as bloating, constipation, or diarrhea, can benefit from reflexology focused on the paw pad regions linked to the stomach, intestines, liver, and pancreas. Gentle circular motions on the center and outer edges of the paw pads stimulate the digestive system, promoting balance and helping to alleviate symptoms. Combine this with the application of gentle heat using a warm towel to enhance relaxation and improve circulation to these areas.

Joint Pain and Arthritis: Many aging pets struggle with joint pain and arthritis, particularly in the legs and hips. Reflexology can help reduce inflammation and improve circulation to affected joints. Focus on the base of the toes and the heel of the paw, which correspond to the limbs and joints. Applying steady pressure with a thumb walking technique on these areas, followed by light circular motions, helps to ease stiffness and improve mobility. Reflexology for joint pain can also be combined with topical treatments like diluted essential oils (such as frankincense or lavender) for additional pain relief.

Respiratory Problems: Pets with respiratory conditions, such as asthma or chronic bronchitis, can benefit from reflexology applied to the center of the paw pad, which is connected to the chest and lungs. Start with slow, circular motions in this area, paying close attention to any tender spots. Applying gentle pressure here can help to open airways and support lung function. Incorporating deep breathing exercises with your pet while doing reflexology can also help calm their respiratory system and reduce stress.

Stress and Anxiety: Reflexology is highly effective in alleviating stress and anxiety, which are common in many pets, particularly those in busy or unpredictable environments. The areas between the toes, linked to the lymphatic system, and the tips of the toes, representing the nervous system, are ideal reflex points for reducing anxiety. By working these areas with light, rhythmic pressure, you can help calm your pet's nerves, reduce tension, and promote a state of relaxation. Pairing reflexology with calming aromatherapy, such as diffusing lavender or chamomile essential oils, can amplify its soothing effects.

Urinary Tract Issues: Pets with frequent urinary tract infections or other bladder-related conditions can benefit from reflexology focused on the heel of the paw, which corresponds to the lower abdomen, kidneys, and bladder. Gentle but firm pressure in this area can help stimulate the urinary system, promote detoxification, and alleviate discomfort. This practice can be particularly beneficial when combined with increased water intake and a diet that supports kidney health.

Reflexology is most effective when used as part of an integrated holistic treatment plan. By combining it with other therapies, such as massage, aromatherapy, and energy healing, you can enhance its benefits and create a more complete approach to your pet's well-being.

Massage Therapy: Before beginning a reflexology session, a brief massage can help your pet relax and prepare their body for deeper healing. Massage also warms up the muscles and improves circulation, making reflexology more effective. Focus on the shoulders, neck, and back to release tension and increase blood flow to the paws, where you will apply reflexology. This combination is especially helpful for pets with musculoskeletal issues, such as arthritis or stiffness.

Aromatherapy: Essential oils can complement reflexology by providing additional relaxation and healing properties. For example, calming oils like lavender or chamomile can be diffused during a reflexology session to help reduce anxiety. For pets with respiratory problems, oils like eucalyptus or peppermint can be diluted and used in a diffuser to support the respiratory system while you focus on reflex points linked to the lungs. However, be sure to research which essential oils are safe for pets, as some can be toxic if not used properly.

Energy Healing (Reiki): Reiki is an energy healing practice that can be seamlessly integrated with reflexology. As you work on the reflex points, you can channel healing energy through your hands into your pet's body, supporting the overall healing process. The combination of physical touch and energy work can deepen the sense of connection between you and your pet while promoting a balance of energy flow throughout the body. This combination is particularly effective for pets dealing with emotional trauma or those undergoing a physical healing process.

Chromotherapy (Color Therapy): Color therapy involves using specific colors to influence your pet's energy and emotional well-being. During reflexology, you can use colored lights or blankets to enhance the effects of your treatment. For instance, blue light is calming and soothing, making it a good choice for anxious or stressed pets, while green light can promote healing and balance. If using chromotherapy, create a comfortable environment by placing colored lamps near your pet during the session or wrapping them in colored blankets to support their healing process.

In addition to physical ailments, reflexology can also be used to address behavioral issues in pets, such as aggression, fear, or hyperactivity. These behaviors are often linked to underlying stress, anxiety, or imbalance in the nervous system. By working reflex points associated with the nervous system, brain, and emotional centers, you can help promote a sense of calm and balance, reducing these behaviors over time.

Aggression: Aggressive behaviors in pets can stem from anxiety, fear, or frustration. Reflexology can help calm the nervous system and promote emotional balance. Focus on the toes, particularly the spaces between them, which are connected to the brain and emotional centers. Light circular motions and gentle pressure on these areas can help reduce aggressive tendencies. Combining reflexology with calming aromatherapy, such as lavender or frankincense, can further support your pet's emotional health.

Fear and Phobias: Pets with specific fears, such as loud noises, unfamiliar environments, or separation anxiety, often benefit from reflexology aimed at reducing anxiety. The areas between the toes and the base of the paw pad are linked to the nervous system and emotional balance. Applying slow, rhythmic pressure to these areas helps soothe your pet's fears and promotes a sense of security. Using reflexology before stressful events, such as thunderstorms or vet visits, can help calm your pet and make them more resilient to fear-inducing situations.

Hyperactivity: Hyperactive pets often have excess energy that can be difficult for them to manage. Reflexology can help calm their nervous system and promote relaxation. Focus on the base of the paw, linked to the digestive and nervous systems, which helps calm the body and support digestion. Applying pressure to these areas can help channel your pet's energy in a more balanced way. Pairing reflexology with regular physical exercise and a calming environment will help manage their hyperactivity more effectively.

To get the most out of reflexology, consistency is key. Regular sessions can help maintain balance in your pet's body and prevent issues from developing. For pets dealing with chronic conditions or behavioral problems, frequent sessions (two to three times per week) may be necessary to see noticeable results. For general well-being, a weekly session may be sufficient.

Monitor your pet's reactions during and after each reflexology session. If they show signs of discomfort or sensitivity in certain areas, this may indicate an underlying issue that needs further attention. Conversely, if they seem relaxed and at ease, it is a good indication that the treatment is working well. Over time, you will develop a deeper understanding of your pet's body and energy flow, allowing you to tailor treatments to their specific needs.

By integrating reflexology into your pet's holistic care routine, you are providing them with a gentle, non-invasive method of promoting health and well-being. With the ability to target both physical and emotional issues, reflexology is a versatile tool that supports the body's natural healing processes. Whether used as a preventative measure or a treatment for specific ailments, reflexology offers a powerful way to enhance your pet's overall quality of life.

In the next chapter, we will explore the concept of multidimensional healing and how various holistic therapies can be integrated into a comprehensive treatment plan for your pet. By combining reflexology, energy healing, aromatherapy, and other modalities, we can create a synergistic approach to health and well-being that addresses all aspects of your pet's physical, emotional, and energetic needs.

Chapter 23
Multidimensional Healing
Integrating Multiple Holistic Therapies

Holistic therapies offer a wide range of benefits for pets, each focusing on a particular aspect of their physical, emotional, or energetic health. While each modality can be powerful on its own, the real potential of holistic care emerges when multiple therapies are integrated into a cohesive healing plan. Multidimensional healing takes a broader approach, addressing not just isolated symptoms or conditions but the pet's entire being—body, mind, and spirit.

At the core of multidimensional healing is the idea that everything in the body and mind is interconnected. When your pet experiences physical discomfort, it can affect their emotional balance, energy flow, and even behavior. By combining therapies such as Reiki, aromatherapy, chromotherapy, massage, and reflexology, we can address these interconnected aspects simultaneously. This approach allows for a more complete and profound healing experience, helping to restore harmony on all levels of the pet's well-being.

In this chapter, we will explore how different holistic therapies can be combined into a personalized, multidimensional treatment plan for your pet. Whether your goal is to maintain general health, address a specific issue, or provide long-term support for a chronic condition, integrating multiple modalities can significantly enhance the healing process.

The effectiveness of multidimensional healing lies in the synergy between various therapies. Each modality complements the others, amplifying their benefits and addressing the pet's needs from different perspectives. For example, while Reiki may help to balance the pet's energy field, massage therapy can release physical tension in the muscles, and aromatherapy can promote emotional calmness. When combined, these therapies work together to create a holistic, integrated healing experience.

Here are some key combinations of holistic modalities and how they can be used together:

Reiki and Massage Therapy: Both Reiki and massage focus on the flow of energy in the body, but they work in different ways. Reiki uses gentle, hands-off energy transfer to balance the pet's energetic field, while massage works physically on the muscles and tissues to release tension. By integrating these two practices, you can address both energetic and physical imbalances at once. For example, start a session with a short Reiki treatment to relax the pet's energy field, then move into massage to release any muscle tension. The combination will leave your pet feeling deeply relaxed, balanced, and restored.

Aromatherapy and Chromotherapy: Aromatherapy, through the use of essential oils, and chromotherapy, which uses colors to influence energy, can both enhance emotional and energetic healing. For instance, you can diffuse calming oils like lavender or chamomile while using blue or green light therapy to create a peaceful environment. This combination works especially well for pets dealing with anxiety or stress-related behaviors. The scent of essential oils interacts with the limbic system, calming the nervous system, while colored light helps to balance the pet's chakras and energy field.

Reflexology and Reiki: Reflexology targets specific points on the pet's paws to stimulate internal organs and body systems, while Reiki works to restore energetic flow throughout the entire body. These two modalities can be combined during a single session to maximize the healing benefits. Start with reflexology, focusing on areas of the paws that correspond to any physical issues your pet may be experiencing, such as digestive discomfort or joint pain. Follow this with Reiki, channeling healing energy into the areas where you felt tension or sensitivity during the reflexology session. This combination can help clear blockages both physically and energetically, leading to a more complete healing experience.

Massage and Essential Oils: Essential oils can be integrated into massage therapy by applying diluted oils directly to the pet's body. Oils such as frankincense, which promotes healing, or peppermint, which can reduce inflammation, can be gently massaged into areas of discomfort. Always be sure to dilute the oils appropriately and consult a professional to ensure that the oils you are using are safe for your pet's species. The combination of massage and essential oils helps to relieve physical pain, soothe the skin, and calm the nervous system all at once.

Breathing Exercises and Reiki: Breathing exercises are a simple but powerful way to calm your pet's mind and body, especially when combined with Reiki energy healing. During a Reiki session, focus on syncing your breathing with your pet's, slowing down your own breath to encourage them to do the same. This practice can help your pet release anxiety and enter a deeper state of relaxation, allowing the Reiki energy to flow more freely through their body. This combination is especially beneficial for pets that suffer from stress, fear, or hyperactivity, as it teaches them to self-regulate their emotions.

To create a multidimensional healing plan for your pet, it's important to take into account their unique physical, emotional, and energetic needs. No two animals are the same, and a treatment plan that works well for one pet may not be as effective for another. Below are some key steps to guide you through the process of creating a personalized, integrated healing approach:

Assess Your Pet's Current Condition: Begin by evaluating your pet's health, behavior, and emotional state. Are they experiencing any physical pain, such as arthritis or digestive issues? Do they show signs of emotional distress, such as anxiety, fear, or aggression? Understanding your pet's current condition will help you determine which therapies are most appropriate to integrate into their healing plan.

Set Clear Healing Goals: Once you have assessed your pet's condition, set specific goals for their healing journey. For example, you might want to reduce your pet's anxiety, improve their mobility, or enhance their overall energy and vitality. These goals will guide you in selecting the appropriate therapies and determining how often to administer treatments.

Choose the Right Modalities: Based on your pet's condition and your healing goals, select the therapies that will best address their needs. For physical pain, massage and reflexology might be the most effective modalities, while for emotional distress, aromatherapy and Reiki might be better suited. You may also choose to include supportive therapies such as chromotherapy or music therapy to create a calming, healing environment.

Determine Frequency and Duration: Each pet responds to holistic therapies differently, so it's important to monitor their reactions and adjust the frequency and duration of treatments as needed. For chronic conditions, you may need to administer treatments several times a week, while for general wellness, once a week may be sufficient. Always pay attention to how your pet responds to each therapy and adjust accordingly.

Create a Healing Environment: Healing is most effective when the environment is calm, peaceful, and free from distractions. When administering treatments, make sure your pet feels safe and comfortable. Use soft lighting, soothing music, and familiar scents to create a relaxing atmosphere. A healing environment supports the effectiveness of the treatments and helps your pet relax and open up to the healing process.

Track Progress and Adjust the Plan: Regularly assess your pet's progress to see how they are responding to the multidimensional healing plan. Are their symptoms improving? Is their energy more balanced? Tracking progress will help you determine whether to continue with the current plan or make adjustments. You might find that certain therapies work better than others, or that your pet needs more frequent treatments for a particular issue.

While holistic therapies can greatly enhance your pet's health and well-being, they should not replace conventional veterinary care. Holistic healing works best when used as a complementary approach, supporting traditional treatments and helping to manage chronic conditions or alleviate side effects. Always consult with your veterinarian before starting a new holistic therapy, especially if your pet is dealing with a serious illness or is on medication.

By integrating holistic therapies with conventional care, you can create a balanced approach that addresses all aspects of your pet's health. For example, if your pet is recovering from surgery, you might use massage and aromatherapy to promote healing and reduce pain, while working with your veterinarian to monitor their recovery. For pets with chronic illnesses like arthritis, reflexology and Reiki can provide long-term relief, while regular veterinary check-ups ensure that their condition is being managed effectively.

One of the greatest benefits of multidimensional healing is that it fosters a deeper connection between you and your pet. Holistic therapies require you to be present, attuned, and sensitive to your pet's needs, which can strengthen the bond between you. As you administer treatments, you will learn to listen to your pet's body language and energetic cues, developing a deeper understanding of their well-being.

This process of connection and attunement not only supports your pet's healing but also brings a sense of peace and fulfillment to you as a caregiver. Healing becomes a shared experience, where both you and your pet benefit from the exchange of love, energy, and compassion.

In the next chapter, we will explore how to take this holistic integration even further, creating a comprehensive healing system for your pet. This will involve adapting therapies over time as your pet's needs evolve, ensuring that their holistic care continues to support their well-being throughout different stages of life.

Building a multidimensional healing system for your pet requires not only integrating different holistic therapies but also adapting these therapies over time as your pet's health and well-being evolve. Pets, like humans, go through various physical, emotional, and energetic changes throughout their lives, and a healing plan that works today may need adjustments to continue being effective in the future. This chapter will guide you through creating a flexible, personalized system that supports your pet's health in the long term, emphasizing how to monitor their progress, modify treatments, and ensure their continued well-being.

As pets age, their health needs change. Older pets may develop chronic conditions like arthritis, diabetes, or kidney disease, which require ongoing management. Additionally, aging can affect their energy levels, emotional state, and even behavior, making it necessary to adjust the types and frequencies of holistic treatments. By being proactive and adapting your pet's healing plan, you can help them maintain a high quality of life well into their senior years.

For example, a young, active dog might benefit from regular massage and Reiki to relieve muscle tension after exercise and balance their energy. As that same dog ages, they may develop joint stiffness or arthritis, which could require more targeted treatments such as reflexology, massage focused on the joints, and aromatherapy for pain relief. Essential oils like frankincense and lavender, known for their anti-inflammatory and calming properties, can be added to the treatment plan to ease discomfort and promote relaxation.

It's important to observe how your pet responds to the treatments as they grow older and make adjustments as necessary. Older pets might require more frequent, shorter sessions, particularly if they have less energy to tolerate longer treatments. They may also respond better to gentler modalities, such as Reiki or chromotherapy, which place less physical demand on the body while still promoting deep energetic healing.

In addition to physical changes, pets often go through emotional and behavioral shifts throughout their lives, influenced by experiences such as moving to a new home, the arrival of a new family member or pet, or the loss of a companion. Emotional stress can manifest as anxiety, depression, aggression, or withdrawal, all of which can impact their overall health. In these cases, it's essential to adjust the holistic therapies to address not only the physical symptoms but also the emotional and energetic imbalances.

If your pet is experiencing anxiety due to a change in their environment, aromatherapy using oils like chamomile or vetiver can promote calmness. Reiki and chromotherapy can help balance the pet's energy field, while grounding exercises, such as spending time in nature or using root chakra healing techniques, can provide stability and emotional security. If behavioral issues like aggression or fear arise, Bach Flower Remedies such as Mimulus (for fear of known things) or Star of Bethlehem (for trauma) can be introduced to help your pet cope with these emotional challenges.

The key to adapting treatments for emotional changes is to remain observant and responsive. Pay attention to your pet's behavior and mood, and be willing to experiment with different combinations of therapies to see which ones have the most positive impact. Over time, you'll develop a deeper understanding of how your pet reacts to stress and what they need to restore their emotional balance.

Consistency is crucial in holistic healing, but so is flexibility. Establishing a regular routine for your pet's treatments can help maintain their well-being, but that routine should be dynamic, evolving as their needs change. The following are some guidelines for creating a routine that adapts over time:

Start with a Baseline Routine: When first developing a healing plan, begin with a basic routine that includes the therapies most suited to your pet's current state. For example, a typical baseline for a healthy, active pet might include weekly massages for muscle relaxation, daily Reiki or energy balancing sessions, and occasional aromatherapy for emotional balance.

Monitor Progress Regularly: Regular check-ins with your pet's physical and emotional health are essential. Keep a journal where you note changes in behavior, energy levels, physical symptoms, and overall mood. This will help you identify patterns and determine when it's time to adjust their treatments.

Be Willing to Modify the Frequency: As your pet's needs evolve, the frequency of treatments may need to change. A pet recovering from surgery, for example, might need daily Reiki sessions to promote healing, which can then be reduced to weekly sessions as they recover. Similarly, a pet experiencing heightened anxiety might benefit from daily aromatherapy, while a pet in a more balanced emotional state might only need it occasionally.

Integrate New Therapies as Needed: As your pet ages or their condition changes, you may find it beneficial to introduce new therapies into their routine. For instance, if your pet develops arthritis, adding reflexology or acupuncture to their existing healing plan can provide more targeted relief for joint pain. If your pet becomes more sensitive to stress, chromotherapy or sound therapy might offer additional support for calming their nervous system.

Incorporate Seasonal and Environmental Changes: Pets, like humans, can be affected by seasonal shifts and changes in their environment. During colder months, they might experience more stiffness in their joints or lower energy levels, which could require more frequent massages or warmth-inducing treatments. Conversely, during times of environmental stress (such as a noisy household or changes in the living situation), you might need to increase calming therapies like Reiki or aromatherapy.

Work with a Holistic Veterinarian: Although you'll be administering many of these treatments at home, consulting with a holistic veterinarian can provide valuable insights. They can help you adjust your pet's plan based on their medical history, current health, and any specific conditions that arise. A holistic vet can also introduce more advanced treatments like acupuncture or chiropractic care if needed.

There are a few key indicators that your pet's holistic healing plan may need adjustment. If you notice any of the following, it might be time to reevaluate the therapies you're using and how often you're administering them:

Changes in Energy Levels: If your pet's energy levels drop significantly or they become unusually lethargic, this could be a sign that their healing needs have shifted. You may need to increase the frequency of energy-balancing treatments like Reiki, or adjust their diet to support their vitality.

Physical Discomfort or New Symptoms: If your pet begins to show signs of physical discomfort, such as limping, stiffness, or difficulty moving, it's essential to incorporate more targeted physical therapies like massage or reflexology. New symptoms might also indicate that their current healing routine isn't addressing an underlying issue, requiring a more focused or intensive approach.

Behavioral Shifts: If your pet becomes more anxious, aggressive, or withdrawn, it's a clear sign that their emotional and energetic balance has been disrupted. In this case, you may want to increase the use of calming therapies such as aromatherapy, chromotherapy, or Bach Flower Remedies, or introduce new techniques like guided meditations to help restore their emotional equilibrium.

Lack of Improvement or Stagnation: If you've been following a healing plan consistently but notice that your pet isn't showing improvement or has plateaued in their progress, it may be time to try different modalities or adjust the frequency and intensity of treatments. Sometimes, adding a new element—like combining sound therapy with Reiki, or introducing reflexology—can provide the breakthrough needed to move forward.

The ultimate goal of multidimensional healing is not just to treat specific ailments but to maintain your pet's overall wellness throughout their life. Holistic healing is a lifelong journey, one that evolves with your pet as they grow and change. By staying attuned to your pet's needs, regularly adapting their treatments, and integrating multiple healing modalities, you can ensure they receive the care and support they need to thrive in every stage of life.

The beauty of holistic wellness lies in its ability to create harmony between the body, mind, and spirit. When you take a multidimensional approach to healing, you're not just addressing symptoms—you're nurturing your pet's entire being. This deep, comprehensive care fosters a sense of peace, balance, and well-being that radiates from the inside out, helping your pet live a healthier, happier life.

As you continue to develop your pet's healing plan, remember to enjoy the process. Healing is not just about the techniques and treatments you use; it's about the connection you build with your pet and the love, compassion, and attention you give them along the way. This journey of healing is a gift you share with your pet, one that strengthens your bond and enhances both of your lives.

Holistic therapies offer a way to enrich your pet's health while deepening your understanding of their needs, allowing you to support them in the most meaningful, individualized way possible.

Epilogue

Now that you've traveled through the chapters of this book, something may have shifted within you. The way you look at your pet probably carries a new depth, a recognition that they are much more than a physical being. You have discovered that by offering holistic care, you are promoting a balance between body, mind, and spirit—not only for your four-legged friend but for yourself as well.

Throughout this journey, you've learned that your pet's emotions are not just reflections of the environment but an extension of your own emotional state. The energy you project—whether of calm, stress, or joy—directly influences their behavior and health. The harmony you create in your own world reflects in every interaction you share. You've realized that healing is a two-way street: by caring for your pet holistically, you are also caring for yourself.

The practices you've explored, such as aromatherapy, chromotherapy, and Reiki, go beyond conventional methods of care. They offer a way to reconnect with the ancient roots of what it means to be a guardian of a living being. The right touch, the soothing scent, the healing colors—all become powerful tools to create an environment where your pet can flourish in full health.

Now is the time to internalize what you have learned. Each practice, each technique, is a seed you can nurture and adapt to your pet's unique needs. The beauty of holistic healing lies in its flexibility and its ability to adapt to circumstances and personalities. There is no rigid formula. There is, however, the sensitivity to perceive what your animal requires and to be present for them in times of need.

At the end of this reading, you now hold not just knowledge but the power to transform your pet's life in a profound way. It is not merely about solving problems but preventing them, creating an environment where healing flows naturally. Your pet will feel it. They will notice that something different is in the air—a space of peace, love, and balance that you have helped to build.

But the journey doesn't end here. The knowledge this book provided is just the beginning. From this point on, the exploration continues. You are now a guardian of wisdom, capable of applying these teachings in daily life, helping your pet not only live with health but with vitality, joy, and serenity.

Allow these practices to continue to grow within you. Refine them, adapt them, and, above all, keep your heart open to your pet's needs. In doing so, you will ensure that every day with them becomes an opportunity for mutual nourishment and true connection. May the energies you share with your little companion bring not only healing but also happiness and fulfillment for both.

And when you look at your pet, remember: they are more than an animal in your care. They are a reflection of your own energy, a being who accompanies you on a journey that is as much about growth as it is about love. May this path always be blessed with harmony, health, and a profound connection that transcends the physical.

Milton Keynes UK
Ingram Content Group UK Ltd.
UKHW042244011124
450424UK00001BA/227